MISSIONS MADE EXCITING FOR ADULTS

CREATIVE IDEAS TO INVOLVE
Adults in Missions

Elizabeth Whitney Crisci

ACCENT PUBLICATIONS
Colorado Springs, Colorado

Accent Publications
4050 Lee Vance View
P.O. Box 36640
Colorado Springs, Colorado 80936

Copyright © 1996 Accent Publications
Printed in the United States of America

Library of Congress Catalog Card Number 96-85475

ISBN 0-89636-330-9

Contents

Introduction

The love of God and an uncompromising desire to worship Him freely brought determined Pilgrims to the shores of America.

The certainty that only the Word of God could change lives for eternity took Adoniram Judson to Burma and William Carey to India.

The compelling whisper of the Holy Spirit drove Mary Slessor into the heart of Africa to tell others that Jesus Christ loved them, died for them, rose for them again.

Martin Luther's unyielding stand at Wittenberg gave the Word of God to commoner and king.

But what are we doing today?

We talk about missions...but few want to give up the "good life."

We have missions weeks...and forget about it the rest of the year.

Where has our passion for telling others about Jesus Christ gone?

Missions Made Exciting for Adults brings that passion back to life. It stirs the minds of twenty-first century adults with the possibilities, their abilities, and gives 60 easy-to-use, interactive ways for today's adults from high school through retirement to make a difference in their world for Christ.

Short term missions, cross-cultural awareness, lifelong commitment, global vision, neighborhood application... these ideas and activities make missions involvement real and personal with 5-15 minute investments. Use them to make missions a weekly priority in the lives of the adults in your church...your Bible study...your Sunday School.

Many churches give to missions. A significant number have missions conferences. Early church missionaries such as Paul, Silas, Peter, James, John, and Barnabas are often the subject of Sunday School lessons for the children and early teens.

But what happens to the adults? Other than occasional speakers, small notes in the church bulletin, or special offerings, missions is no longer a priority or an emphasis in most churches.

Missions Made Exciting for Adults can change that. It makes missions meaningful, a part of everyday life. Christ commanded every one of His followers to be living, breathing, passionate missionaries for Him — at home or abroad. For those who are not called to the sacrifices of overseas missions or Indian reservations, inner city works or rescue missions, there is no holiday. God never releases His people from His command, "Go ye into all the world, and preach the gospel to every creature" (Mark 16:15).

Missions doesn't have to be boring, uninteresting, or an occasional sideline. It can revolutionize and revitalize every aspect of your adult ministry. Make missions exciting, special, life-related. That's what this book is all about.

Your church is Christ-centered, Bible-centered, others-centered. Let your missionaries know that it is also centered on them. That you stand behind them in very real ways.

Are you encouraging short-term missions or presenting the needs of lifelong commitment with global vision and cross-cultural insights? Do the adults in your church know that they are missionaries, too, even if God doesn't call them to a foreign land?

Try these ideas in different classes each week. Make sure that these life-changing ideas are a part of the monthly emphasis of your adult classes. Young adults, the high school group, senior adults, singles, middle adults, every one of your adult classes can discover the life-changing excitement of a commitment to missions — as the at-home support staff so necessary to vital missions work around the world and close to home. It cannot be done as effectively without your church's adults.

There are hundreds of ways to encourage the work of missions through the local church. These 60 creative ideas are a steppingstone that can change your church forever. No ideas have been suggested that use a video camera and tape because many missionaries may not have access to a VCR. If you know your church's missionaries do, then feel free to adapt or create your own activity which would use that medium as well.

God says, "But ye shall receive power, after that the Holy Ghost is come upon you: and ye shall be witnesses unto me both in Jerusalem, and in all Judea, and in Samaria, and unto the uttermost part of the earth" (Acts 1:8). Use these ideas to stimulate the adults in your church to get involved, to consider mission work, to help others carry on His work around the world.

Pray about presenting a variety of missionary projects, themes, socials, and lessons through the 52 weeks of the year ahead. There are so many who have not yet heard about Christ's death, burial, and resurrection. Encourage your church to look outward in concern for the souls of people they don't know as well as those they do know. Let God work to make your church missionary minded, missionary sending, and missionary giving.

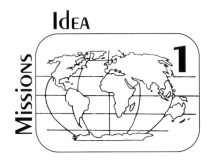

IdEA

Missions

1

PENNIES FOR COWS

PURPOSE:

To show the people within the church how to give specifically and uniquely to meet the needs of their missionaries.

PREPARATION:

Look until you find a place and a missionary that could use a cow in a village. Find pictures of cows. Make penny banks. Make a poster depicting the cow and a village in need as well as the missionary who serves there.

Option: It could be something else that the missionary needs, but make your presentation of the need visual and fun. It may be a snowmobile, ATV, backpacks and hiking boots, a sheep or horse, etc.

Supplies NEEdEd:

❑ Information from missionaries
❑ Pictures of cows
❑ Tin cans or glass jars to use as banks
❑ Glue
❑ Posterboard
❑ Pictures of faraway village
❑ Thick felt-tip pens
❑ Penny rollers
❑ People to count and roll

TimE NEEdEd:

3 minutes the first week
1 minute every two or three weeks for an update
10 minutes several weeks later to collect, count, and praise the Lord

WHAT TO do:

Display the *Pennies for Cows* poster one week before the beginning of the drive. Bring it to the attention of the group on the appointed Sunday and tell how many pennies it would take to buy a cow for the people in the missionary's village in Indonesia or Peru or wherever. If the cow (purchased on the field) would cost $200.00, the need would be 20,000 pennies. In a brief explanation, tell how important the cow would be to the health and the prosperity of the isolated community. Hand out the banks and ask people to get busy saving pennies. Their families can help if they want to make it a family giving activity. After an appointed time (a few weeks), gather the banks and see if there are enough pennies to buy the cow. If not, empty the banks, and send them out a second time. Praise the people for every penny they place in their bank. Every one **counts**.

When the amount is finally reached, sing the "Doxology" together or "To God Be the Glory." Put the ones willing to roll the pennies to work.

Projected Results:

The members of the class will be intrigued, more committed to the missionary cause, and realize they can be involved in many ways. Maybe someone will be interested in going to teach the people how to milk the cow gift!

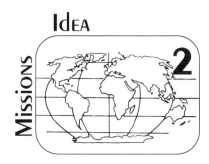

IdEA

Missions

2

Missions Hotline

Purpose:

To maintain awareness of missionaries and up-to-date needs, blessings, and answers to prayer through personal contact.

Preparation:

Get the telephone number of a missionary. Write ahead of time to set a time to call the missionary. Have a microphone next to the telephone or use a speaker phone.

Supplies Needed:

☐ Microphone
☐ Prepared questions ahead of time for the missionary
☐ Telephone
☐ Telephone number of missionary family
☐ Short wave operator, if desired
☐ Large picture of the missionary family blown-up to poster size for the front of the meeting area, optional

Time Needed:

5-7 minutes

What to do:

Arrange for the missionary and his/her family to be available at a certain hour that corresponds to your meeting. (Remember the missionary's family may be in the home country if the missionary is single.) Have someone put in the call a few minutes before the scheduled time in the service. Be sure the conversation can be heard over the microphone. (Sometimes a call can be set up by a ham operator.)

Give some personal background to the missionary about the group and to the group about the missionary.

Then, ask questions and give the missionary an opportunity to respond.

Some suggested questions:
✓ What time is it now where you are?
✓ What is the weather like there?
✓ What did you and your family do today?
✓ What do you and your family do on weekends?
✓ What are your favorite hobbies or recreational activities?
✓ What are some special blessings you're experiencing?
✓ What is the primary focus of your ministry/work and how do you carry it out?
✓ What are the primary challenges you face teaching the people with whom you work about Jesus?
✓ What are the chief products or exports of your country?
✓ Where do your children go to school?
✓ Do you have any special needs?
✓ What personal needs can we pray about for you?

After 5-10 minutes, close the conversation. Have the congregation all say a loud, "Good-bye."

Spend some time in prayer for the missionary.

Option: If you wish, have the people bring in hobby, recreational, school, or ministry materials to send to the missionary and family.

Projected Results:

A keen interest in missions ought to follow. The congregation should feel closer to the missionary and be able to pray with a feeling of more personal involvement for her/him.

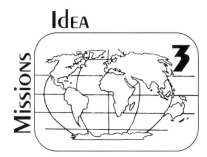

Idea

Missions

3

Cross-Cultural Hospitality

Purpose:

To let the people practice hospitality and see a cross-cultural situation in their own homes, their own church, their own environment, resulting in closer ties to the mission field.

Preparation:

Working through a missionary organization your church already is associated with, find a missionary who would like to send a young person to your home country, state, or province for a semester, for a summer, or for one year in high school. Inform the class and decide which student(s) will be invited. (Depending on your resources or the mission organization's, you may want to bring more than one student to your church.)

Supplies Needed:

❏ A committee to coordinate the overseas student's housing
❏ A church willing to nurture a foreign student
❏ Money to help with in-country travel, clothing, food, etc.
❏ A group of adults who will pitch in and help, be friends with and encourage the student

Time Needed:

15-30 minutes initially
1 semester to 1 year commitment

What to do:

Form a committee to take care of the details: select a host family, find families to help with meals, to take the student on sightseeing trips, to transport the student to school, to sporting activities, to help with finances. Suggest the entire class adopt the student. Take a photograph of the group and the host family with whom the student(s) will stay. Send that to the student and his/her family. Provide all the details and answer the questions the parents will have. Ask for a picture of the student from the parents as well as details on the student's interests and goals for coming.

Meet the overseas student at the airport. Plan a shopping trip to provide him/her with any needed clothing and school supplies. Do an introductory tour of the neighborhood to familiarize him with the area. Try to involve him in youth activities at church. Suggest that each family in your class take him for a meal, to a special activity at school, or some fun program.

Discuss the overseas student in class after he/she has arrived. Talk about the needs, problems, blessings involved in the housing, feeding, adjustment, studies, etc. during the class period. Help the student stay in contact with his family by planning at least one phone call home a week or two after his arrival. For a long-term stay, plan a phone call home at least once a month.

The committee should be aware of difficult situations and even be prepared with alternate housing if the host family becomes unable to continue because of illness or other family situations.

Evaluate the progress of the overseas student and the people involved every few weeks (if it is a long term stay) or every few days (if it is a summer visit). The committee must be ready to step in and help at any moment.

Be sure to saturate the adventure with prayer both in the committee meetings and in the class meetings.

Projected Results:

A mutual feeling of love and care for missionaries, their families, and people of different backgrounds. Create a new sense of closeness to believers around the world as the class gets to know the student and his family's concerns, needs, and more about another country or culture. The personal interaction and involvement in each others' lives should generate a personal identification with those who go on our behalf as the results of our missionary dollars.

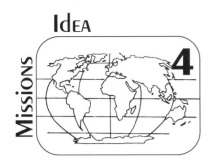

Idea

Missions

4

Try It, You'll Like It

Purpose:

To encourage people to be missionaries right where they are and perhaps encourage some to go somewhere else to serve the Lord.

Preparation:

Make 7 copies of the situations.

Supplies Needed:

❏ Copier (or computer and printer)
❏ Paper

Time Needed:

10-15 minutes

What to do:

Hand out the copies of the situations, then call on participants, one at a time, to present their situation. Probably five or six will be enough, however, seven situations are provided to give the leader some choice.

Situation 1) A neighbor never darkens the door of a church. He does not seem to want to be friendly. What can a Christian neighbor do?

Situation 2) The downtown shelter for the homeless needs servers on Saturday nights. It is in a dangerous area of the city. What should I do?

Situation 3) A missionary in my profession is due home for furlough, but there is no one to replace him. He won't come home unless someone goes. What might I do?

Situation 4) A missionary on home assignment needs a car. She doesn't have money to buy one and no way to get credit. Is there a way I might help?

Situation 5) I would like to be a missionary, and I feel God wants me to serve Him overseas, but I can't stand snakes, spiders, or odd foods. And I've never been able to learn a foreign language. How can I please God and be what He wants?

Situation 6) I have the education but not the "calling" to serve God as a foreign missionary. Why don't I have the desire? Is God as interested in my giving as much as my going?

Situation 7) What is a real missionary? And what is total commitment? Can't I be a real missionary here in my town? Is that enough?

Let the group discuss the situation for several minutes but don't prolong the discussion beyond usefulness.

Projected Results:

A group of adults who are thinking through the whole concept of missions, with the realization that most people are called to be missionaries at home. No one is called to sit back and do nothing; all are called to witness and to support and to pray for those few chosen to go overseas or across the country to serve in a special way. All servants of the Lord are missionaries.

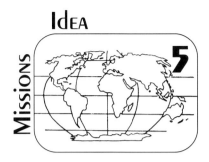

Idea **5**

Missions

WHERE AM I?

PURPOSE:

To give an idea of missions geography, increase understanding, and make a faraway part of the world seem nearer.

PREPARATION:

Collect supplies, select game leaders, find volunteers for refreshments. Use at any church social.

Supplies Needed:

❑ A world puzzle
❑ Pictures of different countries
❑ Small cards
❑ Pins
❑ Pencils
❑ Paper
❑ Foreign refreshments
❑ Pens
❑ Small maps

Time Needed:

2 hours

What to do:

As the guests arrive, give them name tags with continents of the world drawn on them. Each continent (Africa, Antarctica, Asia, Australia, Europe, North America, South America) should be equally divided among the people, because they will form teams for the games. After they pin their name tag on, send them to a big table where they will help make a puzzle of the world.
Games and activities (to be played by teams)

UNSCRAMBLE THE COUNTRY

1—YPEGT (EGYPT)
2—TILAY (ITALY)
3—XMECOI (MEXICO)
4—SSRIUA (RUSSIA)
5—AHNCI (CHINA)
6—LIZRBA (BRAZIL)
7—GNNUIEEAW (NEW GUINEA)
8—NNGLDEA (ENGLAND)
9—OAPLND (POLAND)
10—RGAENTIAN (ARGENTINA)

SPELLING BEE TEAMS

(The team can work together for correct spelling, but once a spokesperson says the letters, it is a final try. Add more countries if you wish.)

1) VENEZUELA
2) CHILE
3) ALBANIA
4) ZAIRE
5) TAIWAN
6) COTE D'IVOIRE
7) INDONESIA
8) ECUADOR
9) NEPAL
10) COLOMBIA
11) ISRAEL
12) THAILAND

WHO'S WHERE?

(This activity can be done individually or in teams.) Make a list of the church missionaries in a lefthand column. Make a list of the countries where they serve in a righthand column, but not in order. Photocopy the master list and give one to each person present. Ask the teams or individuals to draw lines from the missionary to the country where they serve. The first team or person to finish with the correct answers wins.

WHERE AM I?

Collect pictures of other countries from magazines; mount them on construction paper. Number the pictures. Pass the pictures around to the different teams. Participants are to figure out the country. After five minutes, collect the pictures. Show them one-by-one and give the correct answers. The team with the most right answers wins.

WHAT CAN I DO?

Give each team paper and pencil. At the count of three, let them list as many things as possible that they think missionaries would need and/or things they could do to help the missionaries. The team with the longest list wins.

LANGUAGE BARRIERS

1) If I am speaking Cantonese, I would be in _____? (China)

2) If I am speaking Swahili, I would be in _____? (East Africa or Zaire)

3) If I am speaking Portuguese in South America, I would be in _____? (Brazil)

4) If I am speaking Afrikaans, I would be in _____? (South Africa)

5) If I am speaking Bantu, I would be in _____?
(Central and southern Africa)

6) If I am speaking Amharic, I would be in _____?
(Ethiopia)

7) In Austria, I would speak _____? (German)

8) In Guatamala, I would speak _____? (Mayan, Spanish, English)

9) In Pakistan, I would speak _____? (Urdu)

10) In Taiwan, I would speak _____? (Chinese)

11) In The Netherlands, I would speak_____? (Dutch)

12) In Nepal, I would speak _____? (Nepali)

DEVOTIONAL
Sing several rousing missionary songs, have a missionary speaker, if possible, or ask the pastor to bring a short missionary challenge.

REFRESHMENTS
Try to have some homemade foreign pastries.

Projected Results:

Stimulate curiosity about the world, the language challenges, the people who need to hear the gospel. Group members will realize the size of the world and the huge challenge for missions that it entails. They may feel more involved and enjoy the fun and good fellowship.

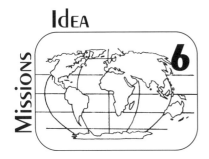

Idea

Missions

6

Coffee Hour Special

Purpose:

To encourage people to know, to understand, and to get absorbed in missions.

Preparation:

Select a home that could be used for a special or occasional coffee hour. Find missionaries who are available and willing to speak to a small group. Make invitations and give them out to people in the vicinity of the house—both church people and neighbors. If you have a college nearby, see if they have international students from the missionaries' countries. Extend a special invitation to them. They may be homesick and greatly enjoy talking with someone from home and/or seeing pictures of their country.

Supplies Needed:

- ❏ Coffee cake
- ❏ Doughnuts
- ❏ Coffee
- ❏ Tea
- ❏ Paper plates
- ❏ Napkins
- ❏ Cups
- ❏ Invitations
- ❏ Willing host and/or hostess
- ❏ 3-5 missionaries
- ❏ One refreshment which is native to one country, optional

Time Needed:

30 minutes to plan;
1 1/2 - 2 hours at the Coffee Hour

What to do:

Plan a *Coffee Hour* when there are missionaries available during a missions conference or when several

church missionaries are home on furlough. Morning is preferable, but afternoons work out as well. Serve the coffee and goodies to the guests. (You may want to serve at least one dish native to one country represented.) After 30 minutes of getting to know one another, ask everyone to sit down and allow each missionary to speak briefly—not more than five minutes. Let them discuss one of three things:
1) Their family
2) Their work and the people
3) Prayer requests

Then open up the session to questions. The guests can direct their question to an individual or to all three missionaries. Try to make the time informal, the answers short, and keep the question time fast-moving. Perhaps the leader can start the talk-fest by asking each missionary to quote John 3:16 in the language they are working in or share a scary experience. Then ask for questions.

Finally, close the time with prayer and suggest any further questions be directed to the missionaries individually who will gladly remain for a few more minutes. Thank the hostess and think ahead to another coffee hour in a few months.

Option: If you invite foreign students, plan ways to continue to build friendships as an at-home foreign missions outreach.

Projected Results:

A group of believers who have a personal relationship with missionaries, curiosity from non-believers, and a real awareness of what God is doing today on the mission field. Potential for an ongoing missions emphasis and friendships with foreign students.

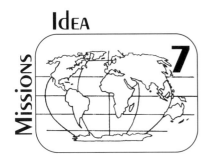

Idea

Missions

7

MK Adoptions

Purpose:

To involve adults in the lives of missionary children via regular letter writing, card sending, small gifts, and especially prayer.

Preparation:

Compile a list of all the children of all the church-supported missionaries. Find pictures of the children, birthdays, ages, school situation, and addresses. Place all the information for each different child attractively on a 3" x 5" card.

Supplies Needed:

❏ 3" x 5" index cards
❏ Pictures and statistics of missionary children

Time Needed:

5-6 minutes the day *MK Adoption* is presented
a 30 second reminder once a month
continuing prayer for a specific child each class period

What to do:

Involve an adult Sunday School class, a Bible study group, a breakfast fellowship, or any and all small groups in the church.

Use an enthusiastic person to present the idea of adopting a MK (missionary kid). Explain that it will mean several things.
1) To pray for the child.
2) To write to the child on a continuing basis, whether or not they receive an answer in return.
3) To send a special card and inexpensive gift at birthday and Christmas.

4) To encourage the child at school events with "congratulations" at promotion or graduation, for sports achievements, to offer encouragement in school. Present all of the missionary kids affiliated with your church. Let the class select a MK for adoption. Some may want to individually "adopt" a child, so more children will be included.

Once a month, ask people to report about the adopted MK and encourage them to continue in the process. Explain how much it means to a child so far from their homeland and grandparents and cousins. Praise the people for their good work and faithfulness.

Projected Results:

A keen interest in missions, as well as MKs, will develop if the people follow through. All children love to get mail. Missionary children will feel an "extended family" relationship which will reduce their cultural isolation.

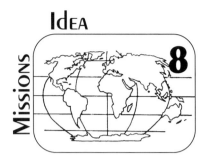

Idea

Missions

8

Missions On Location

Purpose:

To help people understand the importance of prayer and their personal support of the missionaries.

Preparation:

Make four copies of the skit and select outgoing, enthusiastic people to portray the characters in the skit. Prepare a poster to display in the church foyer at least a week before the skit as well as the day of the performance.

Supplies Needed:

- ❑ Platform or stage
- ❑ 4 volunteers to be skit characters
- ❑ 4 copies of the skit
- ❑ Plants
- ❑ Artificial fire
- ❑ Posterboard and paints
- ❑ Picture of jungle and tribal village blown-up to backdrop size, optional

Time Needed:

5-7 minutes

What to do:

Make the platform look like a jungle village. Use artificial plants, a grass hut, artificial fire. Those portraying characters should read the skit ahead of time, but practice is not really necessary if they are good readers. Be sure they know that they must be able to project loudly enough so the congregation or group can hear them.

SKIT: "Alone In The Jungle"

Characters: MISSIONARY DOCTOR, WIFE, SON, NATIVE

Missionary Doctor: What a day! I can't believe the problems.
Wife: What do you mean?

Doctor: There was a lion ready to attack me on the path to the church. The woman I took blood samples from last Friday is worse today, and I don't have the results of the tests back so I can't really treat her. I'm only easing the symptoms. The tribe's witch doctor came to the clinic and threatened me with his spear, telling me my medicine was trickery.

Son: Dad, come quick! There's a snake in the bedroom.

Doctor: Oh no! Hand me that rifle. Where's the baby?

Wife: In the crib. Hurry.

Son: It's in the corner, or it was a moment ago.

Doctor: There it is, heading for the crib. Pray.

Wife: Dear Lord, help my husband kill the snake. Please keep our baby safe.

(Loud bang.)

Son: You got him! You hit him right in the head. He's dead.

Doctor: Praise God. What could possibly happen next.

Son: Why do these things happen if people back home are praying for us?

Doctor: Sometimes people forget to pray because we are so far away. Sometimes God wants us to trust Him and He sends these situations to help us grow in Him. It's not always because people aren't praying for us.

Wife: We're not guiltless on the need to pray. I promised to pray for the pastor at our home church. But do you know, I haven't been faithful to do that. Sometimes several days go by, and I don't pray for him, his family, or our church at home.

(Loud knock at door.)

Native: Friend, I need you. My wife is very sick!

Doctor: Oh, no! It's the lady I'm trying to diagnose. I'll come right now. I'm afraid we won't have time to talk tonight, dear. I must run. Where's my medicine case?

Wife: Here. Hurry! We'll be all right.

Doctor: Oh no. Son, I'm sorry I won't have time to spend with you tonight.

Native: Hurry, my friend. Run fast. My wife very sick.

Doctor: I'll try to keep up with you. *(They disappear off the platform.)*

Wife: Come, Son. Let's pray for your father. *(She bows her head.)* "Father, we thank you for taking care of us here in this place to which you've called us. We know you want us here. Please be with my husband right now. Give him the wisdom to know how to treat this dear native lady who is so close to trusting you as Savior.

Father, how we need the prayers of those at home today. Thank you for those who pray for us. We know you hear their prayers, and we could not stay here to serve you without their support.

But you hear my prayers, too. Heal this sick woman, Lord. She has three little children, and they need her. And if she were healed, others might come to believe in Jesus. We need you to heal her so the witch doctor cannot say our medicine killed her. We trust her to your care. I pray in Jesus' name. Amen!"

The wife sits at table and notices a letter on it.
She opens it.

I can't believe I've been so busy today I did not even open this letter from dear old Sadie.

Son: Is Sadie the older lady who let us stay in her home last year when we went back to the States?

Wife: Yes. She has always had an open heart for us even though we didn't really know her well. She has been such an encouragement. She really helps us feel connected to our church. Here, I'll read her letter outloud.

"Dear Missionary Friends, how I wish I could send some money to help you in your work. But you know how limited my income is. All I can do is pray. I felt burdened to pray for you especially hard today. I prayed for protection against wild animals. And I prayed for a miracle that would bring many in the village to Christ. Let me know how God is answering these prayers. Lovingly, Sadie"

Son: Wow, Mom! Can one person's prayers make so much difference? Does God really help people pray that specifically for us?

Wife: Yes, He does...your father's home! How is the woman?

Doctor (tired): She'll be all right now. She had a high fever. Lots of cool water and aspirin will do the trick for tonight. Tomorrow, we will take her to the medical clinic in the capital. We'll be gone at least three days, but I don't want to wait any longer. We'll make sure that the infection won't return.

Wife: I'm so glad God answers prayer. Look dear, this letter came today.

Family gathers around father as he takes the letter.

Projected Results:

The congregation will realize how important their prayers are to those who go overseas to a foreign mission field. Many will want to pray daily and make that commitment. Idea can be used in any Sunday service, missionary conference, or other gathering of church adults.

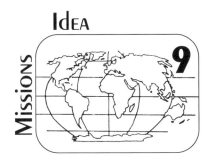

IDEA 9

Missions

MISSIONARY MATCH

PURPOSE:

To inspire people to get acquainted with, pray for, write to, and be interested in the missionaries supported by the church.

PREPARATION:

Prepare a missionary quiz with questions about church missionaries. Copy it onto postcards or letters, along with an invitation for everyone to come to the next meeting. Mail the cards seven days before the meeting.

Supplies Needed:

❑ Copier (or computer and printer)
❑ Cards
❑ Information about the church missionaries
❑ Bookmark or other simple award for each participant

Time Needed:

At home—10 minutes;
At the meeting—10 minutes

What to do:

Select questions about church missionaries that won't be impossible to answer, but will be helpful for the people to know. Choose one of the three suggestions listed below.

Birthdays
Match the birthdates with the right missionaries.

1. July 23	a. John Parsons
2. March 1	b. Louise Brown
3. January 30	c. Dick Allen
4. April 11	d. Jennifer Schultz
5. September 21	e. Don Olsen
6. December 5	f. Bob Rogers

Countries
Match the missionaries with the right countries.

1. Zaire
2. Peru
3. Alaska
4. Philippines
5. Pakistan
6. Argentina

a. Dick Allen
b. John Parsons
c. Bob Rogers
d. Don Olsen
e. Louise Brown
f. Jennifer Schultz

Spouses
Match the spouse in the left column with the correct spouse in the right column.

1. Bob Rogers
2. Don Olsen
3. Jennifer Schultz
4. Dick Allen
5. Louise Brown
6. John Parsons

a. Phyllis
b. Caroline
c. Ron
d. Gary
e. Donna
f. Elinor

Provide a bookmark or some simple award to all who answer the quiz correctly. Try a different quiz again in a few months.

Option: Send a party in a box for anniversaries and birthdays. Provide the balloons, paper plates, napkins, cups, party hats or other items (candles and a nice paper tablecloth, etc. for an anniversary).

Projected Results:

An awareness of the location, the family, the birthdays or other information about church missionaries, showing that the missionaries are real people who need prayer and attention.

IdEA

Missions

10

FiNd THE MissiNq LiNk

Purpose:

To show the participants that they are the *Missing Link* in successful missionary service.

Preparation:

Copy the quiz.

Supplies Needed:

- ❑ Copier (or computer and laser printer)
- ❑ Paper
- ❑ Pencils
- ❑ Lap boards or table

Time Needed:

5-6 minutes

What to do:

Distribute the *Find the Missing Link* Quiz to all the students. At the count of three, they are to circle every word beginning with the letter "P."

Find the Missing Link Quiz

Missionaries are **p**eople who serve the Lord wholeheartedly at home or abroad. We must **p**ray for them every day. Sometimes missionaries feel very alone, because no one writes to them and very few **p**ray for them. When they go through a crisis, they have no regular, daily **p**rayer support or anyone else to listen. The same kinds of work-related stress or co-worker **p**roblems you face, they encounter. When they are homesick, there is no one to encourage them. When they have difficulty with the language, danger from wild animals, or endure **p**hysical illness, who is **p**raying for them? When unbelievers try to harass them, who is kneeling before the throne, asking God to give them strength and wisdom? When a holiday comes, who cares that there is no holiday for those on a foreign field? Who is standing in the gap, fighting the power of Satan, bridging the weaknesses that besiege every believer by interceding with God?

Missionaries need many things for their work to prosper. The most important is prayer. Obviously, they must have financial support, but they need prayer more. They need people to witness to, but they can only do that through the power of prayer. They need supplies, but those come through Christians who give and pray that they can be delivered. Whether believers are serving the Lord in our city or abroad, they need prayer. If they are serving God in our state or on a foreign field, they need prayer. If they have answered a call to full-time missions service in our country or faraway, they need prayer. If they are taking the Word of God to others on our continent or across the ocean, they need prayer. The missing link for success on all and every mission field of the world is **Prayer.**

After the group circles the words beginning with 'P,' ask them what the words are. Then ask the discussion question: "What can we do about that?" See if they can think of 10 ways to be the missing link in each situation. Close with prayer for God's wisdom and help for continued and regular prayer for missionaries.

Projected Results:

An awakening of the class to the need for their prayers and an increase in believing prayer for the work of individual missionaries that the church helps to support.

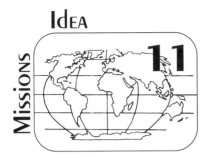

IDEA

Missions

11

Good Jokes to Go

PURPOSE:

To encourage missionaries and their families by bringing a light touch to their lives. To provide a unique evening of fellowship and missionary-centered fun for your adults.

PREPARATION:

Send out cards and announce in the church bulletin or newsletter that there will be a *"Joke"* party. To come, people must bring a funny, clean, interesting or true-to-life cartoon or written joke cut from the newspaper or hand-copied from a book. (No photocopies.) Set the time and the place. Bring a dozen or so extra jokes to add to the collection. Provide the address of church-supported missionary(ies).

Supplies Needed:

- ❑ A committee to plan and host the party
- ❑ Postcards
- ❑ Mailing list with addresses of class members
- ❑ Stamps
- ❑ Jokes and/or cartoons
- ❑ A home in which to meet
- ❑ Refreshments
- ❑ 4 small prizes
- ❑ Information and address for one or more of the church missionaries
- ❑ Paper (plain and construction)
- ❑ Glue or staples

Time Needed:

A 2 hour party

What to do:

Select a committee to plan and execute a *Good Jokes to Go* party. The entrance fee is a clean joke, written out or in cartoon form. After everyone arrives at the party, have guests read or tell their jokes. Put the cartoons together in whatever categories or order you want. Glue or staple them onto sheets of paper. Cover with construction paper and title the book. For instance: *Good Clean Jokes from Our Church.* Give prizes for:

1) the funniest
2) the most true-to-life
3) the most profound
4) the cleverest

Let the people vote on the winners of the categories after all the jokes have been read. Give a brief biographical sketch about the family, including where they serve, their particular type of service, and their family.

End the evening with a devotional on the Bible verse, "A merry heart doeth good like a medicine: but a broken spirit drieth the bones" (Proverbs 17:22).

Have refreshments and fellowship together as you share the joke books. Select a special person to mail it/them to pre-selected church missionaries.

Projected Results:

The group will have a lot of fun and laugh-filled fellowship. They will enjoy sending such a personal, enjoyable gift to a missionary family. The party may be so successful that it will become an annual (or semi-annual) affair!

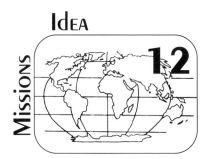

Idea

Missions

12

Memory Bank

Purpose:

To place God's Word, especially verses which emphasize missionary work, into the memory of the adults in the local church so that they will know God's expectations of their lives concerning missions.

Preparation:

Select a dozen missionary-related Bible verses. List them on posterboard. Option: Illustrate the verses for easy memorization as explained below.

Supplies Needed:

- ❑ Posterboard
- ❑ Thick felt-tip pens
- ❑ Copier (or computer and printer)
- ❑ Paper

Time Needed:

5 minutes for a series of four meetings

What to do:

Announce one week in advance: *Next week we begin taking charge of our own investments by making deposits in our Memory Bank. Come and enjoy while you learn.*

Print a list of about a dozen missionary verses. Some suggestions:

Matthew 28:19-20	Mark 13:10	Mark 16:15,20
Luke 24:46-47	Acts 1:8	Acts 16:9
Acts 26:17-18	Revelation 14:6	Malachi 1:11
Psalm 2:8	Psalm 22:27	Psalm 96:3
Hebrews 9:27	Romans 10:14-15	
Isaiah 6:8	I Peter 1:17-25	

Let the adults select four verses that they would like to learn. At each meeting for four sessions, use a visual to teach the verse. Cover-ups are one way to learn. Have the entire memory verse visible to begin with. Ask the group to read the verse with you twice. Cover-up one word and read it again. Cover-up two more words and read it again, etc. until the whole verse is covered. By that time, with continuous repetition, they should all know the verse.

Continue with the rest of the meeting. But, before the final "amen," repeat it again. Pass out the list of verses to be learned and continue the process with a new verse the following week. After four weeks, give each participating adult a real bank with the words, *Memory Bank*, taped to it and the four verses. Ask them to put their change in it for a month and bring it back for a special missionary project.

Option: If you have any artists in your group, have them illustrate the verses. You could also have class members look for pictures which would illustrate each word or a group of words.

This idea works well in any informal fellowship from Bible studies, adult and youth Sunday School classes, missionary rallies and/or conferences, evening services, coffee hours, fellowship suppers, and even prayer meetings.

Projected Results:

God's Word, hidden in the hearts of His people, always bears fruit. Some adults may volunteer to serve the Lord on the mission field, for either long or short term trips. Some adults may begin giving more money for the work of missions. Most will have the need of missions underscored in their lives and remember for a long time God's expectations of each believer toward His work and in the lives of those who need to hear about salvation.

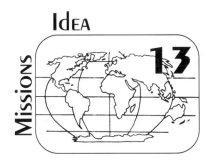

Idea

Missions

13

Prayer by Candlelight

Purpose:

To help believers spend more time in specific prayers for specific missionaries. To bring believers to a sense of personal responsibility and awareness that the mission fields need more workers.

Preparation:

Test how much of a candle burns in 10-15 minutes, depending on the desired time for prayer. Mark another candle at the proper point. Make a list of specific missionary prayer requests and copy them, one per person.

Supplies Needed:

❑ Test candle
❑ Copier (or computer and printer)
❑ Candle and candle holder

Time Needed:

10 minutes (15 if desired)

What to do:

At an appropriate time during a prayer meeting, explain that the candle will be lit, and it will burn until the prayer time is over. Give each person a list of specific missionary prayer requests. If convenient, divide the group into small groups of five or six to pray together. Read Matthew 9:35-38 aloud. Then ask someone to light the candle and let the people pray in specific sentence prayers for specific needs.

Ask God to convict others of the needs in various fields and to call missionaries. Ask God to speak to each heart in your group about their personal involvement in missions, their willingness to go and/or give. To close the prayer time, ask a pianist to play softly when the candle reaches the 10-minute mark.

Close the session with a prayer hymn like: "The Doxology" (Thomas Ken), "Praise the Savior" (Thomas Kelly), "Blest Be the Tie That Binds" (John Fawcett), "Bring Them In" (Alexcenah Thomas), "I'll Go Where You Want Me to Go" (Mary Brown), "We've a Story to Tell" (Colin Sterne), "Send the Light" (C.H.G.), or "To God Be The Glory" (Fanny Crosby).

Projected Results:

People will take the responsibility of praying for missionaries more seriously; they will put their own hearts and lives and commitment on the line, and they will realize that prayer isn't easy. It takes work and time.

Spelling Bee-Yond

Purpose:

To familiarize the group with the missionaries the church helps to support so that they will remember to pray and support them.

Preparation:

Make a list of church missionaries and the places where they serve.

Supplies Needed:

❏ None

Time Needed:

5-8 minutes

What to do:

Ask for six volunteers. Divide the volunteers into two teams divided by sex, age, side of room, color of hair, or any other way feasible. Explain the rules: a name of a missionary is said outloud. Team 1, Contestant 1 tries to spell it. If correct, the team gets 100 points. If incorrect, Team 2, Contestant 1 gets an opportunity. If correct, that team gets 50 points plus the next word to spell. If incorrect, the leader should spell the word and Team 2 gets a new word (name of another missionary) to spell. Use about 12 words (names). Make the list personal for the local church. For example:

1. M E C K L E N B U R G	2. S M I T H
3. R E I N E R T	4. L L O Y D
5. L U C E	6. W O O D B U R Y
7. Y O U N G	8. S T A P L E S
9. S T R O U P	10. R A Y C H A R D
11. H O F F M A N	12. M I L L S

The next time the *Spelling Bee-Yond* is used, try a list of places where your church missionaries serve. Or use the place of service as a Bonus Round or Bonus points with the names as they are spelled.

1. Botswana	2. Harlem
3. Afghanistan	4. Zaire
5. Philippines	6. Belize
7. Navajo Reservation	8. Ecuador
9. French Guiana	10. Ukraine
11. New Guinea	12. Mexico

Congratulate the winning team, encourage the losing team, and promise another session in a month or two.

Use this idea in informal services like evening services, mid-week prayer meetings and/or Bible studies or other small group meetings.

PROJECTED RESULTS:

Generates team spirit and provides a fun way to remember the names of missionaries and their places of service. Should encourage more prayer, more giving, and more concern for those who serve around the world.

Missions

BEFORE THE BELL

PURPOSE:

To encourage people to discover their potential in missions and to remember that they are missionaries.

PREPARATION:

None

SUPPLIES NEEDED:

❏ Blank pieces of paper (or 3" x 5" cards)
❏ Pencils
❏ Timer

TIME NEEDED:

5 minutes

WHAT TO DO:

Distribute the paper or cards and the pencils to everyone in the group. Ask the group to number 1 - 10 down the left side of the paper. Explain that at the clap of the leader's hand, they are to begin to list 10 things they can do for missions.

One or two suggestions might help - like pray for missionaries, visit a mission field, give extra money. Remind them that since every Christian is a missionary, they can include things they can do in their own neighborhoods, companies, state or province.

Set a timer for three minutes. When the bell rings at the end of the time, collect the papers, mix them up, and give them out again, people should end up with one that is not their own. Ask everyone to read the paper they receive.

Close with prayer that each one will seek at least one new way, perhaps several ways in which they can be become more involved in missions.

PROJECTED RESULTS:

People will realize there are several areas where they can become more involved in the work of missions. They will also be reminded of their responsibility to witness for Christ where they are. Foreign countries are not the only mission fields.

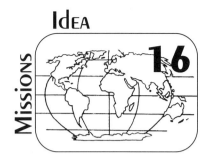

IdEA

Missions

16

Sunday Travelogue

Purpose:

To keep the church people up-to-date on the missionaries' activities, problems, needs, prayer requests.

Preparation:

Gather prayer letters and personal letters from the different missionaries that the church helps to support. Select a few enthusiastic people to prepare and share geography plus exciting news to share with the church people.

Supplies Needed:

☐ At least 4 volunteers
☐ Missionary prayer letters
☐ Up-to-date geography information
☐ World map, optional
☐ Foam core board, optional

Time Needed:

Less than 5 minutes during the service

What to do:

Ahead of time, select several enthusiastic people who are willing to present the *Sunday Travelogue*. They need to share geographical information about the place where a particular missionary is serving and condense a letter from a missionary serving there. Emphasize the health and blessings of the family, the problems, needs, and prayer requests. It ought to be about four minutes and then that same person should lead the congregation in prayer for the people of that country and the chosen missionary family. Use one *Sunday Travelogue* each Sunday for three or four weeks.

If you have a world map, mount it on foam core board and display it at the front of the room, pointing out the location of the country. Facts of interest to also include would be the time difference between that place and the time of your service, any other items of interest such as weather, exports, political or geographical significance.

Be sure to have current information available for the people who will do the presentation, and be sure the person condenses and puts the information in his/her own words with a sense of delight.

Projected Results:

An educated congregation with a world-wide view of God's work and a sense of their involvement in getting the gospel out to a world in desperate need of the Savior.

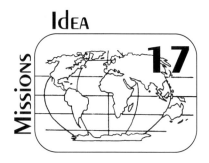

Idea

Missions

17

World-View Placemats

Purpose:

To learn about missions while making the placemats and to have a take-home reminder for through-the-week remembrance.

Preparation:

Gather the desired information for the placemats. Make a sample and gather materials.

Supplies Needed:

❑ Large roll of paper, freezer paper works well, 12" x 18" pieces
❑ Copier (or computer and printer)
❑ Felt-tip pens, variety of colors
❑ Missionary information/Prayer cards
❑ Clear plastic or clear shelf paper
❑ Rubber cement
❑ Map of world
❑ Scissors (crimping sheers will add a nice edge)
❑ Magazines, optional

Time Needed:

30 minutes in meeting
fellowship time for use of placemats
a long time at home

What to do:

Plan a time for the group or Bible study to make placemats for a coming fellowship dinner or coffee hour. Provide statistics, missionary names and addresses, missionary birthdays, pictures from magazines if available, map of the world showing location of missionaries, or whatever the group would like to place on placemats.

Glue (rubber cement is the best) the copied information on the large paper (or write it on the paper in colored markers). Add an interesting design, prayer, missionary quote, or whatever will make the placemat attractive and worth keeping. Carefully cover the finished placemat with a piece of clear plastic shelf paper. Smooth out and trim around the edges. Make enough placemats for the number of people attending the coming function. Or, provide the supplies and have those who come to the activity come at least an hour early and make their own placemat.

Making placemats is a good idea to use in a women's meeting or small group Bible study; use the placemats at a banquet, pot luck supper or coffee hour.

Projected Results:

There will be great interest in the coming dinner; there will be much excitement about the information on the placemats. The dinner will focus people's attention on local church missions. The placemats will be taken home, and missions, hopefully, will become the center of many meals.

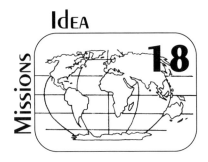

Idea

Missions

18 VALENTINES FOR MISSIONS

PURPOSE:

To show love to those on mission field assignments in a tangible way.

PREPARATION:

Gather materials for making valentines. Get a list of church supported missionaries' names and addresses. Make a couple of samples.

Supplies Needed:

❑ Red, pink, and white construction paper
❑ Paper doilies
❑ Valentine stickers
❑ Plain paper
❑ Felt-tip markers
❑ Scissors
❑ Glue
❑ Names and addresses of missionaries
❑ Envelopes
❑ Stamps
❑ Dried flowers, ribbons, optional
❑ Polaroid camera, optional

TIME NEEDED:

15 minutes

WHAT TO do:

Place all the supplies on the tables for people to use. Show a couple of samples.
Idea: Put a fancy heart on the cover and the words: *Happy Valentine's Day.* On the inside, glue a piece of blank paper and include a short, newsy, handwritten letter and a Valentine verse or poem, Bible verse, and the signature of the sender. On the back include a

Polaroid picture of yourself, the group, the church, or personal artwork, stickers, or another Bible verse about love and why you appreciate the work the missionaries are doing.

Be sure to put the valentines into an envelope, seal and address it. Stamp it with proper postage. A volunteer can take the valentines to the post office the next day. Close the session with prayer for the missionaries who will receive the valentines.

A good time to use this idea is after an evening service or prayer meeting, at an adult fellowship or social, or in a Sunday School class.

Projected Results:

A personal connection with specific missionaries and a reassurance to the missionaries that their service is recognized and appreciated.

Idea

19

Missions

Stamp Club

Purpose:

To encourage the people to write to the missionaries they help support and to share their letters with their friends in the fellowship.

Preparation:

Make booklets to be distributed to the congregation. Each page should say:

Country ＿＿＿＿＿＿＿　　Missionary ＿＿＿＿＿＿＿

Four pages should be enough. Prepare and place a list of six or eight church missionaries and their addresses on the back page. Leave space to add stamps from the missionary's letters. Print or write *STAMP CLUB* on the cover along with a place for the owner's name.

Supplies Needed:

❑ Paper
❑ Copier (or computer and printer)
❑ Addresses of church missionaries

Time Needed:

5 minutes the first week
2-3 minutes once a month for six months

What to do:

Distribute the *Stamp Club* booklets to the entire group during the Sunday morning "Missionary Moment" or "Announcement" time of the service.
Have an enthusiastic letter writer explain the process.

Please select one or two missionaries to correspond with. Write to them on a regular basis, whether or not you get a reply. Tell them about activities at church, share family experiences with them, ask them to pray about special concerns of your family or your church. An air letter is least expensive, but one sheet of paper in an envelope is inexpensive as well.

When people receive an answer, ask them to steam off the foreign stamp, attach it to the *Stamp Club* booklet, and be prepared to share the booklet and the letter at church. Eventually, the booklets can be displayed on a bulletin board. Encourage the people to pray for the missionary's needs.

This is a good idea to use in Sunday morning services, mid-week services, or any continuing programs at the church.

Projected Results:

The people will form a new habit of writing to their missionaries, getting involved in their lives, learning more about life on a mission field, and keeping missions a vital part of their church lives.

Idea **20**

Missions

Missions Bouquet

Purpose:

To get people to intercede more for missionaries. To bring a unique missions emphasis to the morning and/or evening service or at a missions conference.

Preparation:

Prepare a bouquet of silk flowers with names of missionaries printed on tags and attached to each flower. Cover a special vase (or a tall can) with a map of the world. Place the empty vase on a table in the front of the church and the flowers on the pulpit.

Supplies Needed:

❑ Silk flowers
❑ Felt-tip pen
❑ Tags with strings
❑ Tall vase or can
❑ Glue
❑ World map
❑ Names of church-supported missionaries

Time Needed:

2-3 minutes each Sunday for a month or two

What to do:

During a special missionary moment in the church service, a lay person or the pastor can pick up a flower with the name of a missionary on it and place it into the missionary vase. Identify the missionaries and their families, then pray specifically for them. The prayer might be something like this...
Dear Father, we pray today for the Jones family serving you in Zaire (or wherever they are). We know they have had a hard time with language (or health, or schooling

for their children, or whatever the need is). We ask that you will encourage their hearts today. Give them strength to meet all their needs this day and may they be assured of our continued prayers both here in our service and later in our homes.

Thank you for these dedicated, special people you have called and led into this place of service. Help us to be faithful in our support of them as we honor you and your work. In the name of Jesus, Amen.

Two missionaries per week could be used to speed up the *Missions Bouquet* process, placing two flowers in the vase and asking two people with strong voices or with a roving microphone, to pray for them.

On the final Sunday, ask people who will promise to pray regularly for the particular missionaries to come after the service and take one flower home with them as a continuous reminder.

Projected Results:

The emphasis on intercessory prayer will touch hearts in many positive ways. The people will realize that missions is a continuing program of prayer and giving that requires their ongoing commitment, not a once-a-year conference.

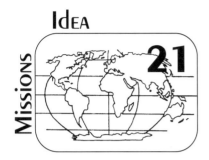

Idea

Missions

21

REASON SEASON

PURPOSE:

To let people think through their own reasons for not serving the Lord full-time at home and/or for not going to the mission field. Perhaps they will realize their reasons for not witnessing or giving to missions are actually excuses.

PREPARATION:

None

Supplies Needed:

❏ Paper and pencils
❏ Table or lap boards
❏ A small prize

Time Needed:

5-6 minutes

What to do:

Announce:
Jesus said, "Go ye therefore, and teach all nations, baptizing them in the name of the Father, and of the Son, and of the Holy Ghost" (Matthew 28:19).

Ask: *How have we obeyed that verse?*
Ask people to share what they have done to fulfill the Great Commission. Then ask them to see, in the next three minutes, how many reasons (*aka* excuses) people have given for not going to the mission field or for not witnessing in their neighborhoods or work places. The adult with the highest number of reasons (excuses) before the time limit wins a prize.

Give the command, "Go!" After three minutes, have them put their pencils down and count their reasons.

Ask the one with the most to read their list. Others can add different excuses to the list. Make no judgments, but repeat Matthew 28:19 before dismissing the class or going on with the next activity of the day.

This idea works well in small group meetings where the participants know each other - perhaps an adult Sunday School class, a home Bible study, or when a larger group breaks up into small groups.

Projected Results:

The class ought to draw the conclusion that they have been guilty of some of the reasons (actually excuses) mentioned. Perhaps they will realize that reasons are too often our excuses and are not valid before the Lord. This is not meant to be a guilt trip, but an eye opener.

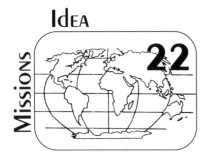
COME ON BOARD

PURPOSE:

To increase the scope of the mission outreach of the local church to include the neighborhood, the urban areas, across the country, as well as the ends of the earth.

PREPARATION:

Make or find a large, approximately 24" x 30" picture of a large passenger train. (Try a travel agency.) Glue the picture onto heavy posterboard or corrugated board. (Rubber cement works best.) Print the words, "Come on board!" at the top. Select a person with a dedicated spirit to share the following message for three weeks. (If you wish, substitute a picture of a cruise ship/ocean liner.)

Supplies Needed:

❏ Posterboard, at least 24" x 30"
❏ Thick felt-tip pens
❏ Large picture of a train, to fit on the 24" x 30" poster
❏ Rubber cement or glue
❏ Individual to present "Come on Board!"
❏ List of mission opportunities and needs
❏ Flyers about short-term missions
❏ Regular pens
❏ Large picture of a cruise ship/ocean liner to fit on the 24" x 30", optional

Time Needed:

5 minutes during the church service the first week
3 minutes the next two weeks

What to do:

Make the "Come on board!" poster and place it on the easel. The first week, have it in the front of the sanctuary or meeting room. After that, place it in the foyer. Have the selected person use the following information and present it, enthusiastically (preferably in one's own words) to the church body for three consecutive Sundays.

First Sunday:

"I invite you to take a train trip with me. We are going around the country and the world in our imaginations. As we travel, we'll ask our missionaries what they need. I think they will tell us that they need Christian books and videos, clothing, food for hungry people, money to buy essentials, translation skills, prayer helpers, carpenters, medical assistants, secretaries, teachers, house parents, transportation drivers, farmers, agriculturists, doctors, pilots, mechanics, friends, churches committed to missions awareness.

Some of us could go overseas right now and help. Some of us can give more money to purchase the things needed in foreign countries or here at home. Some of us can go down the street and befriend our neighbors and be a missionary to them. Some of us can go into jails or homeless shelters and minister.

We need money and volunteers right here in town, too. Will you go into our city and help at the mission? Will you go into the neighborhoods and help those who may never speak to you or ask for help? All of us can "Come on board" the missionary train and and serve somewhere, somehow. Will you "Come on board?"

This poster says, "Come on Board!" That means God wants you! If you'll be part of missions here where we live and part of the worldwide missions effort, will you sign your name? If you put your name on this poster, you will be saying that you will get involved in missions. The poster will be here after the service. Think about it before you sign your name and make your commitment. It won't be a promise to me or to this church. It will be your promise to God. How much is your word worth? He'll be depending on it—and on you.

The speaker should pause and sign it right then in front of the congregation. Then pray.

Second Sunday

Repeat most of the information. Give the people who didn't have a chance to sign the poster last week an opportunity to sign it as they leave. Mention that it is in the entry way for their convenience.

Third Sunday

Repeat the information as necessary. Especially aim toward the young adults, telling them they can have a ministry for God via short term projects, financial gifts, prayer, witnessing to friends. Remind them of the location of the poster.

Follow-up

The pastor might preach on witnessing the following Sunday to keep the missionary spirit active. Make mission society literature available as well as information on short-term projects and a list of missionaries and their needs. Give time for follow-up testimonies from those who have gotten involved in their neighborhoods or in other ministries.

This idea involves the entire church body. Everyone can decide to accept their responsibility to get involved in missions via a campaign for signing up to do something special in a local missions outreach. It might be ministering to the unchurched widow down the street through physical labor or cleaning her house. It might be volunteering as a tutor in an inner city project. It could be an open home for an unwed mother. But everyone can have a mission work.

Projected Results:

A missionary-minded church with most of the congregation excited about going, about giving, about praying, and about helping. Many will become involved in ministries they may not have considered. The reports will encourage the entire congregation as they begin to see God's results.

Idea

23

Music & Signatures to Go!

Purpose:

To keep the congregation and missionaries in close touch with each other; to give missionaries reminders that they are loved and supported; to know the needs of missionaries and to pray for them.

Preparation:

Have supplies handy and plan a couple of testimonies about what getting mail means to them and how your volunteers have been encouraged by letters. Have at least one person tell what music means to them.

Supplies Needed:

❑ *Thinking of you* cards
❑ Pens
❑ Addresses of several missionaries
❑ Stamps
❑ Music cassettes, optional
❑ Padded mailing envelopes, optional

Time Needed:

10-15 minutes during a missionary program, an adult fellowship supper, Bible study, or Sunday School class

What to do:

Announce, enthusiastically, "We are sending cards (and music) to three (or more) of our missionaries. Please sign the cards as we send them around the room. Also, include a line or two of greeting."
Suggest a few greetings they might use like:
"We're praying for your native translator to be saved."
"I was encouraged by reading Psalm 89:1 today. Hope you will be, too." *"We trust God is giving you mental and emotional strength for your work and good*

friendships with your co-workers." "May your ministry be blessed with much progress this week." "Remember us? You ate Sunday dinner with us when you spoke at our church. Wish we could be there for dinner with you."

Address the envelopes and put stamps on them. Select someone to drop them off at the post office right after the meeting. Be sure you have the right amount of postage for foreign air mail if needed.

Have three people pray for the three missionaries.

Option: Have everyone bring a music cassette to include with the letters. Send one or two per letter.

Projected Results:

A continuing and renewed encouragement to missionaries the church has sent out. A continuing and renewed realization of the group's part in bringing the gospel to those who need it. Perhaps a continued interest in writing to those far from home for the sake of the gospel.

IDEA

Missions

24

Identify the Picture

PURPOSE:

To keep the members in the local church praying for, acquainted with, and deeply concerned for the missionaries they support.

PREPARATION:

Gather prayer cards from all the church missionaries. Cut out the pictures of the missionaries and mount them on posterboard. Number the pictures, but do not include any names.

Supplies Needed:

❑ Missionary prayer cards
❑ Posterboard
❑ Paste or rubber cement
❑ Papers
❑ Pencils
❑ Felt-tip pen
❑ Easel, optional

Time Needed:

6-8 minutes during a social gathering

What to do:

Keep the poster covered. Distribute paper and pens. Ask the group members to number their papers from 1 to 10 (or however many pictures you have on the poster). Then uncover the poster and ask them to go to the poster and identify the pictures by writing the names of the missionaries beside the correct number on their paper. Be sure to allow time to give the correct answers. Have someone write the missionary's name under the picture as the picture is identified. Then the poster can be displayed for several weeks to continue its ministry of keeping the missionaries in the limelight.

This activity would be a good one to do before *Music and Signatures, Please!*

Projected Results:

A new awareness of the church-supported missionaries followed by a new sense of closeness and identity with them.

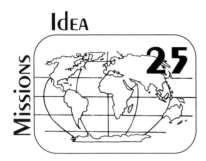

Idea

Missions

25

Half a Letter

Purpose:

To get the people excited about missions—excited enough to pray, to give, and to get involved in the lives and needs of the missionaries.

Preparation:

Find a very exciting missionary letter, one that tells a scary experience. Talk with the pastor about using it in a church service and plan the time and date.

Supplies Needed:

❑ A scary letter from a church supported missionary
❑ A person with a strong voice
❑ Travel brochures, optional

Time Needed:

3-5 minutes on two consecutive Sundays

What to do:

After selecting an alarming letter, find the most dramatic place to stop. Have a pre-selected person read the letter during the "Missionary Moment" in the service. He/she should read the letter and stop at the designated place. Announce: "The letter will be finished next week". Then the reader or the pastor should pray for the missionary family.

The following week, at the same time slot, finish the letter with a brief introduction for those who missed the previous week. Pray again for the missionary family. It might be a good follow-up for the pastor to use the experience in the letter as an illustration in his sermon.

Option: Have travel brochures to the mission fields where the church missionaries are working available and displayed on a table.

Projected Results:

The people will realize that there are hard times on the mission field and they should be concerned enough to pray regularly, to write regularly, and maybe even go for a short term to help the missionaries. Suggest they pray about taking their annual two-week vacation to a mission field where they become the missionaries' helper-servant.

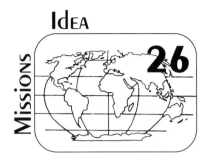

Idea

26

Midnight Prayer

Purpose:

(1) To challenge adults to spend time joined together in prayer for the missionaries they know and/or their church supports. (2) To promote the awareness of and continual prayer for missionaries and their needs in a Bible class, a prayer group, or any small group within the local church.

Preparation:

Find a volunteer to coordinate the *Midnight Prayer*. Make a large poster and a challenge card with the same information, designating a special prayer date and time for members of the group. Make a list of missionaries and needs for each.

Supplies Needed:

❑ Posterboard
❑ Felt-tip pens
❑ Cards with the theme and the prayer requests
❑ People willing to participate

Time Needed:

3 minutes the first time it is presented
60 seconds once a month to pass out cards and encourage people to remain committed

What to do:

Contact each of the church missionaries by letter at least two-three months before you plan to begin the *Midnight Prayer* project. Tell them what you want to do and ask them to respond with specific needs they have for which your group can pray by a date at least two weeks before the project. Encourage them to share family needs, physical, and spiritual needs. Let them know that this is a personal connection of Christian brothers and sisters who share "Family" ties. Personal identification with similar needs and people will help your group maintain their faithfulness in praying and make the people for whom they are praying more real.

Ask someone with a real missions enthusiasm to challenge the group to spend individual time in prayer at midnight, once a month, for the special needs of the church missionaries. Make up a poster and individual cards with the title *Midnight Prayer*. Display the poster, and on it list five specific needs of church-supported missionaries. Then ask for volunteers who will commit to pray for a few minutes (at home) at midnight once a month for these people and needs. Distribute the cards to the volunteers.

Remind the people that the purpose is to have the class united in prayer at midnight on (for instance) the first Friday of every month. Each will pray from their own home, but each will be united before the throne of God with the same prayer requests. Each month the leader of *Midnight Prayer* ought to have 60 seconds to share new cards, with new requests on the last Sunday of the month, making the very first day of the new month *Midnight Prayer* Sunday. This will mean this leader will have to assume the responsibility of staying in touch with the missionaries.

A good time to plan to begin this is the last Sunday of December, making *Midnight Prayer* a New Year's Resolution.

Projected Results:

A missions-focused group of people, growing together as a class and as Christians, united in prayer, beseeching the Lord for definite requests of missionaries. Encourage reports on answers to prayer and continued correspondence with the missionary families.

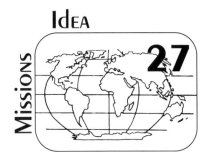

Idea

27 LANGUAGE BARRIERS

PURPOSE:

To help the people realize that learning a new language can be difficult and present a significant problem, especially in view of the missionary's desire to present the gospel and/or help the people.

PREPARATION:

Find several people who can communicate in another language. If missionaries are available, use them. Find a foreign language Bible or a Bible story book in a foreign language.

SUPPLIES NEEDED:

❏ Foreign language Bible (or Bible story book)
❏ Microphone
❏ Several who speak another language
❏ Questions to ask
❏ Overhead projector, optional
❏ Transparency with questions written in foreign languages, optional

TIME NEEDED:

5-8 minutes

WHAT TO DO:

Ask two people who speak another language to come to the platform or to the front of the meeting room. Have them say, *"What would you like to know?"* in a foreign language. But they should look at the interviewer. Then have the interviewer ask questions like:

How do you like being in the United States?
Do you know that we pray for you?
Have many people come to Christ?

What is the hardest part of being a missionary?
Will you read John 3:15-17 for us?
Will you lead us in prayer?
What can we do to help you?

Each question will be answered in the other language. Ask both foreign speakers the same questions. Finally, ask them to say a few words in English about the difficulties they have had with the language.

This idea works well during a church service Missionary Moment or at a missionary conference or coffee hour.

Optional: Have your foreign language volunteers write the questions on the transparency in their language so group members see how hard it is to learn to write as well as learn the spoken language of the people group.

Projected Results:

The people would get a feeling of the frustrations and language difficulties missionaries face on the field and see a need to pray for these needs.

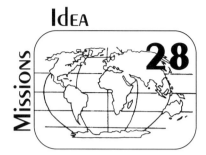

IdEa

Missions

28

LET'S GO!

PURPOSE:

To encourage the people to be missionaries at home. To teach them that they are not exempt from or immune to Jesus' Great Commission.

PREPARATION:

Search out three different ministries that could use volunteer help within a 10 or 20 mile radius of the church. Make an attractive poster for each of those ministries and place sign-up sheets under each one. Display these posters in the front of the church. Place an announcement in the Sunday bulletin for two weeks prior to the service.

Supplies Needed:

❑ Publicity material from local Christian organizations
❑ Posterboard
❑ Felt-tip pens
❑ Paper
❑ 3 volunteers to make the posters

Time Needed:

A few minutes (perhaps 5, do not prolong it), after the pastor's sermon.

What to do:

Work with the pastor, selecting a time when his sermon presents the people with their obligation to be servants of Christ and challenges them to make a commitment and investment of their time and lives in the lives of others as examples of Christ-like service.

Point out the many service opportunities available in your community or through your church outreach programs to the homeless, alcoholics, drug addicts, to nursing homes, jails, a housing project with Neighborhood Bible Clubs, to Awanas, MOPS, children's church, shut-ins, a home for unwed mothers, Habitat for Humanity, or whatever is a current need in your area or your church.

Before the service, place the poster at the front of the church. With the pastor's involvement, three enthusiastic people make a plea for three ministries that really need help. Identify the organization and its purpose, explain why their involvement one night (or day) a month would really help in presenting a faithful testimony of Christ, in bringing souls to the Lord, and/or leading new Christians into a growing faith. Encourage them to come forward during the closing hymn and sign up to serve. Perhaps there could be an extra sign-up sheet for 'where most needed' to help those who do not have a preference.

Be sure, after the presentation, that someone takes over the planning, assigning, and using of these volunteers. A chairperson for each organization should be selected to help the new recruits get involved, set a time, and plan transportation to the facility.

Getting people to sign up isn't enough. They also need to be led into the actual service. Some people will even need someone to go with them the first time. A team of workers, rather than individuals, often works better (unless someone wants to help with something like accounting or secretarial skills).

A few weeks later, ask for testimonies from those who became involved in the *Let's Go!* sign-up.

This idea works well as an emphasis in any church service that has a service emphasis.

Projected Results:

A new awareness of the mission fields within reach of individual Christians in the local church. They can each be missionaries in some Christ-honoring outreach project.

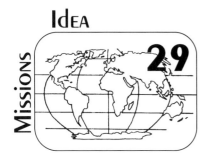

Idea

Missions

29

CONTINUOUS LETTER

PURPOSE:

To encourage people to write letters to missionaries and show them that it is not hard, boring or expensive.

PREPARATION:

Purchase a few air letters, or get several sheets of writing paper, envelopes, and overseas airmail stamps. Have recent letters from two or three missionaries along with their addresses. (It is best to have names of missionaries known by the group). Provide lap boards or a table to write at, along with a few ideas of what could go into a letter.

Supplies Needed:

❑ Writing paper
❑ Envelopes
❑ Overseas stamps or air letter forms
❑ Pens
❑ Lap boards or table
❑ Letters from missionaries
❑ Addresses of missionaries

Time Needed:

5-10 minutes

What to do:

Use this idea at a women's or men's fellowship, after an evening service, at a church social, at a coffee hour, or a Bible study.

Show recent letters from missionaries. Read a paragraph from each one and suggest that the people should write a letter back to those missionaries. One paragraph, two or three sentences from each person attending will be enough. Suggested subjects to write about might be: tell who they are, their occupation, their family members, and a praise to the Lord or a Bible verse to share. Pass the letters from one person to the next one on the right, until all have an opportunity to write to several of the missionaries. Be sure to put the letters in envelopes, address, and mail them right away. Explain that missionaries are very busy people. It may be months before they get a letter back, but be sure to share the answer as soon as it comes. Spend a couple of minutes in prayer for the missionaries who will receive the letters.

Projected Results:

The people will get enthused about missions. They may begin writing letters on their own to missionaries. They will pray more intelligently for the missionaries; they will possibly entertain missionaries when they come back to the church on furlough, and may be burdened to give more to missions.

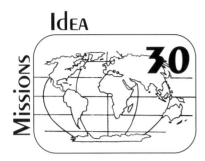

IdEA

Missions

30

Send Help

PURPOSE:

To show the believers that they can help in a concrete way. To give the missionaries concrete fulfillment of a need and reassurance that they are supported and cared about by those at home.

PREPARATION:

Get a letter or telegram with a specific and immediate need from a missionary. Make a poster for the *Send Help* theme with the specific need pictured. Recruit a person with true missions enthusiasm.

Supplies Needed:

❑ Posterboard
❑ Felt-tip pens
❑ Pictures
❑ Name of home or foreign missionary with an immediate need
❑ The need in writing (letter or telegram)

Time Needed:

Approximately 8 minutes plus follow-up time

What to do:

When a specific need reaches someone on the missionary committee or the pastor's desk, or someone concerned about missions, discuss it, and see if there might be items the people could help purchase. Make a poster revealing the need.

Good projects for this *Send Help* might be: Sheets and pillowcases, canned goods for a church food pantry, office equipment for a Christian organization, school books or athletic equipment for an MK (missionary kids) school, etc. If items are used, they must have at least one year's use left in them. No old, useless items!

Ask the people to give the needed item within a week. Specify a specific place to put the items as they are brought in. Select a committee to pack and send the items that are brought in.

Follow up the project by giving a report on the total amount given and the benefit it was to the missionaries involved.

Projected Results:

People will feel a sense of involvement as they help meet an urgent need.

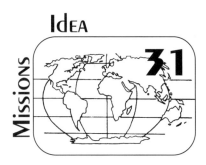

IdEA

Missions

31

Circle Thoughts

Purpose:

To encourage Christians to openly express opinions about missionary subjects.

Preparation:

Have a prepared list of Circle Thoughts, perhaps the list suggested here or a more personalized list from your local church needs.

Supplies Needed:

❑ A circle of chairs for the participants
❑ Bell

Time Needed:

Approximately 8 minutes

What to do:

Have the group sit in a circle. Appoint a bellringer. Explain that each person is to make a comment, one short sentence concerning the subject suggested to them. There is no right or wrong statment, no judgment on the person's opinion or observation. Everyone just suggests a short thought to add to the conversation.

Ideas for Circle Thoughts are:
1) If I were to go to the mission field, I would want to go to _____.
2) The best way we can help _____, our missionary, is to _____.
3) Missionaries need money because _____.
4) I can be a missionary, right here in this town, by _____.

5) If I wrote to a missionary, I would encourage them and their family about _____.

6) If I had the opportunity to encourage a young person to be a missionary, I would do so by _____.

7) If someone gave me $10,000 and asked me to invest it in missions, I would _____.

8) When I pray for a missionary, I should pray for or about _____.

9) If I could spend a month on a mission field, I could help by _____.

10) If there is no gospel witness in my neighborhood, I could make that my mission field by _____.

If anyone extends their sentence or says more than two sentences, the bellringer rings the bell to cut them off. If short statements aren't used, Circle Thoughts loses its effectiveness.

This idea works well in small group Bible studies, Sunday School classes, women's missionary fellowship groups, men's breakfasts, or wherever a group of 20 or less meet.

Projected Results:

People will say things that will astound the group. Even quiet people will enter in. Leaders will discover ways that the group can get involved in home missions and overseas ministries. The group will see places and ideas others have about missions. Group members will get to know one another better. Some may be motivated to follow through with their thoughts.

Idea

Missions

32

Amen!

Purpose:

To encourage the people to get excited, interested, and active in hearing the message of missions and witnessing.

Preparation:

None, except, if desired, make a placard that reads: A M E N ! Ask the minister or missionary speaker to prepare a message on missions at home and abroad.

Supplies Needed:

❏ AMEN placard, optional

Time Needed:

1 service; however long the speaker preaches

What to do:

Discuss the "A M E N !" procedure with the speaker and ask him to use the word "missions" many times during his message. Just before the message, explain to the congregation that every time the speaker uses the word, "missions," the people are to say "AMEN!" During the message by the pastor or the missionary, the congregation should say "Amen" often at the beginning of the message and then ease off as the message progresses. Ask a few key people to say "Amen" at the proper time, to encourage others to keep the process going.

Optional: To help them, the assistant in the pulpit can hold up the A M E N ! placard at the appropriate times.

Projected Results:

The congregation will be involved; they will pay attention and hear the message. All ages will be involved in the missions challenge.

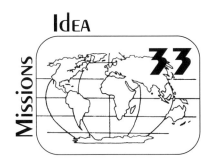

Idea **33** Missions

Costumed Announcement

Purpose:

To make information unforgettable and encourage people to come to the banquet, conference, or prayer meeting.

Preparation:

Find a person willing to dress in native garb and willing to share about missions and to invite the church to a missions special.

Supplies Needed:

❑ Costume, authentic or homemade, but very similar to the actual clothing of the people and country of missions emphasis

Time Needed:

3 minutes at most

What to do:

Select a person willing to dress up. If that person isn't a dynamic personality, have him/her stand up front during the announcement made by someone else who can attract attention.

Have the person enter from the rear of the auditorium and march up the center aisle to the platform as if he/she owns the place. The pastor should question his/her appearance to identify what is happening, then announce an upcoming missionary banquet, a missionary conference, a missionary prayer meeting, or whatever might center on missions for a night.

The announcement might be like this:
"UMBA...LUUMMA...MY ENGLISH IS NOT TOO GOOD, BUT I NEED YOU. WEDNESDAY NIGHT AT 6:00 PM IS

BANQUET. THERE WILL BE MUCH TALK ABOUT MY COUNTRY AND YOU WILL LEARN ABOUT THE NEEDS OF MY PEOPLE. OUR MISSIONARY, JOE JONES, WILL SPEAK. WILL YOU COME? PLEASE? UMBA...LUUMMA!

The pastor can reiterate and encourage attendance.

Projected Results:

The unusual announcement will get the people excited about the upcoming event and help them remember to come. They will be able to ask questions and talk to someone fresh from the mission field and will be encouraged to keep on giving and praying.

Idea

34 Shopping Spree for MKs

Purpose:

To encourage the people to take a concrete interest in the children of church-supported missionaries. To provide encouragement to the children of missionaries.

Preparation:

Select a missionary family with children. Make a poster with their names, ages, and where they live. Secure two clothing catalogues from which they can choose new things to wear.

Supplies Needed:

❑ Picture of missionary family
❑ Names and addresses of missionary children (MKs)
❑ Posterboard
❑ Felt-tip pens, variety of colors
❑ 2 clothing catalogues (e.g. Penney's, Sears, Land's End, etc)

Time Needed:

5-6 minutes the first week
several weeks in-between for corresponding with the young people while concurrently spending 1 minute for successive weeks to raise the money to buy clothing for the young people.

What to do:

With the approval of the class, select a missionary with children (including teenagers). Place the poster with their statistics (names, address, ages, field of service) in front of the class. Explain to the class the first Sunday:

"Most MKs have hand-me-down clothes and rarely get to shop in stores like ours. We want to send them these two catalogues and give these young people the freedom to pick out any two pieces of clothing they want. We will raise the money to purchase these items for them and send the clothing to them. We'll start giving now, and when we have enough money, we will purchase the chosen items, and get them in the mail."

Keep the class up-to-date with the progress of the project and remind the group how much they or their children like new clothes. Tell them how much it will mean to the missionary parents and boost their morale. Along with the money and, eventually, the clothes, spend time in prayer for the whole missionary family!

Projected Results:

A new and sustained interest in this one missionary family. An outpouring of love that will spill over into happier missionary young people serving with their parents overseas. A group of people at home who re-learn the joy of giving.

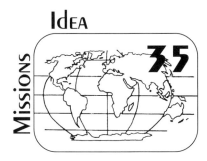

Idea 35

TESTIMONY TIME

PURPOSE:

To help people know the missionaries better, how God called them, and how they came to know the Lord as Savior.

PREPARATION:

Write to four or five church-supported missionaries and ask them to respond with their testimony. Ask them to respond on tape, if possible, or on paper. Wait enough weeks to get the answers back.

Supplies Needed:

❑ Missionaries' names and addresses
❑ Writing paper
❑ Envelopes
❑ Stamps
❑ Tape recorder
❑ Tape
❑ 1-5 volunteers to write the letters

Time Needed:

15-20 minutes each to write the letters
10-15 minutes within any church service

What to do:

The questions to ask the missionaries are:
1) How and when they came to know the Lord as Savior.
2) How and when they were led of the Lord to become a missionary.

Ask them to respond on audio tape if possible, otherwise via a letter. Perhaps the letter writer(s) could correspond with several home missionaries as well as foreign missionaries.

When the answers come back, set a date to share the responses with the pastor and the missions committee. Advertise the Testimony Time two weeks in advance.

Before the service, adjust the tape recorder to the microphone so all can hear. Announce: "We have a personal word today from our missionaries. First, Jon Jones, serving as a mission pilot in Thailand." (Play the tape or let someone read the letter. Quickly move to the second letter or tape when the first is finished. Announce only the name of the missionary, the mission work (church planting, pilot, house parent, secretary, accountant, translator, etc.) and the country of service. Go on to the third and the fourth.

Do not be tempted to comment on the testimonies; they speak for themselves. Then have a prayer of thanksgiving for the people of that country to hear and understand the message of salvation and for the Lord's continuing work in the lives of their missionaries (mention by name).

Projected Results:

A fascinated church body with a renewed realization that the missionary's testimony is not that much different than the average Christian. And that the call to the mission field is seldom a spectacular event, but usually comes from a heart that is listening to God and willing to obey.

IDEA

36

I Can't! I'm Afraid!

Purpose:

To show people that serving the Lord in dangerous places need not be scary because the Lord is on their side.

Preparation:

None

Supplies Needed:

❑ Willing participants

Time Needed:

5 minutes

What to do:

Select two groups of participants, 2-5 in a group. The participants stand in two groups, one on the left side of the room, one on the right. The two groups banter back and forth.

Group 1 (in unison): There is a need for people to serve a meal at the inner city mission on Friday night.
Group 2: I can't! I'm afraid.
Group 1: There is a need for people to go door to door in the new development.
Group 2: I can't! I'm afraid.
Group 1: We need volunteers to go to Mexico City to help build a church.
Group 2: I can't! I'm afraid.
Group 1: We are going to an Indian reservation to teach Vacation Bible School. We need volunteers.
Group 2: I can't! I'm afraid.
Group 1: The missions committee has asked us to double our commitment to missions for this next year.

Group 2: I can't! I'm afraid.
Group 1: There's a family in the projects that is hungry. We should bring them baskets of food tomorrow.
Group 2: I can't! I'm afraid.
Group 1: We need a Bible Club for the children on the south side of the city. We need two teachers.
Group 2: I can't! I'm afraid.

Interrupt the two groups and add, "These are not our needs today, but we will face similar ones soon. Are we ready or are we afraid to serve God where He may call us?"

Quote Isaiah 41:10: "Fear thou not; for I am with thee: be not dismayed; for I am thy God: I will strengthen thee; yea, I will help thee; yea, I will uphold thee with the right hand of my righteousness."

Close with prayer.

Projected Results:

Believers will realize that fear is not a God-given excuse. It comes from His enemy and ours, Satan. Many will realize that there are areas close at home where they can serve. They will be better prepared to answer a call for a service project.

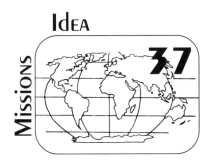

IDEA

Missions

37 **A Halfway Home Church**

PURPOSE:

To give people a serious, life-changing challenge to be intimately involved and reach out to offer help on a local mission field. To help people see that there are many ways to fulfill the Great Commission.

PREPARATION:

Print out the words to the "Committed for Jesus" song on a large posterboard.

Supplies Needed:

❑ Posterboard
❑ Thick felt-tip pen
❑ Music for "Jesus loves Me"
❑ A volunteer to organize the project
❑ Volunteers willing to train and be involved
❑ Professional counselor willing to train the volunteers
❑ A church willing to be involved intimately in the lives of people who need long-term help, an extra investment of love

Time Needed:

10-15 minutes, first week
5 minutes of prayer about the project for several consecutive weeks before the commitment is made and the project launched
6 months or more if project is adopted

What to do:

You will need to check with the pastor first and possibly meet with him, the church attorney, and a Christian counselor to determine liability and insurances needed before presenting this idea.

Place the words to the "Committed for Jesus" song in front of the congregation or the group. Have someone sing this song through once.

"Committed for Jesus"

(tune: "'Jesus Loves Me," music by William B. Bradury)
Jesus needs me, this I know,
For the Bible tells me so;
There is work that I can do;
It's commitment time for me and you.

Chorus:

Yes, Jesus needs me, yes, Jesus needs me,
Yes, Jesus needs me, the Bible tells me so.

Ask the group to sing the song together. Then spend a few minutes explaining what the words mean through an outreach that will require a prayerful commitment.

"I'd like to suggest that we prayerfully consider making an outreach to our local mission field of recovering drug addicts and alcoholics. Let's make our church a halfway house/home of help and encouragement.

"We can offer our help to clients leaving rehabilitation groups or clinics. We can offer our church as a group 'family' and 'home' to the Christian counselors in our area and our volunteers as the ongoing helpers people trying to change their lives often need."

Arrange with a professional counselor to present a sample session which non-professionals can use to help individuals. Ask for volunteers who are willing to be trained to give counseling and support for a six month period to one person. Arrange to set up your own hot-line so there is a pre-established life-line available for them to grab onto. You may want to arrange group sessions to role play ways of coping with life that don't include drugs or alcohol.

Sing the song again. Ask the people to consider the proposed outreach project prayerfully. It will require long-term commitment, lots of love, and people who really have a heart and burden for this special mission field. Set a date at least 3-4 weeks in the future when you will ask for a silent ballot so that no one feels any group pressure to agree to a program to which they are not personally convicted to be committed.

If the group agrees to become a halfway home for recovering addicts, implement the program by asking for a dedicated leader/organizer who will carry it through.

Alternative: If this is not a viable situation for your church, change the emphasis so that the church people are challenged to sign up to volunteer at an established city, state, or county halfway house. Talk with any Christian counselors in your church to see if there are private clinics who need volunteers. Encourage volunteers to adopt one recovering addict and make that person their special mission field. They may be able to help the person find a job, include him or her in their home activities, give spiritual counsel, pick the person up for church services and activities, and/or include the person in a group Bible study.

Alternative: Change the emphasis to a children's home or a children's hospital. Ask for volunteers who will "adopt" one child and invest time and love on him or her and, in the case of a hospital situation, in the lives of the parents. This may be especially meaningful if you live in a metropolitan area where parents must go for specialized treatment and live away from home and other children or their spouse.

Projected Results:

Songs often have more memory retention than words. The tune and the words may come back as a reminder through the week that Jesus expects us to use our time to serve Him. The program will be an ongoing outreach into a very needy mission field surrounding the local church body.

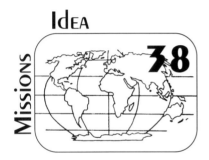

38 Coffee & Prayer Break

Purpose:

To let people see how important prayer for missionaries can occur any time, anywhere.

Preparation:

Get a late-breaking prayer request from a missionary.

Supplies Needed:

- ❑ A bell
- ❑ A prayer request
- ❑ A loud voice

Time Needed:

3-4 minutes

What to do:

During a regular coffee or refreshment hour, while people are mingling with friends, ring a bell. With a loud voice, announce, "We have just received an urgent prayer request from our missionary, Don Westinghouse in Zaire. His daughter is very ill. If we can just be still for one minute, we will ask _____ to lead us in prayer for this one request."

The prayer ought to be short, specific, and prayed loudly, so all the people can hear without a microphone.

Encourage the people to remember this need at home, then go back to the coffee break.

Projected Results:

The people will sense a serious call to pray for special requests from missionaries. Most of them will also remember to pray at home.

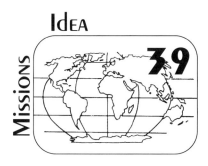

Idea

39

Missions

Always First

Purpose:

To help each adult evaluate where his or her priorities are in different aspects of their lives.

Preparation:

Make copies of the activity sheet so there is one per person or arrange to have it placed in the church bulletin.

Supplies Needed:

❑ Copier (or computer and printer)
❑ Paper
❑ Pencils
❑ Church bulletin, optional

Time Needed:

As a group activity, about 10 minutes

What to do:

As an insert in the bulletin, make a brief announcement. "There is a questionnaire inside your bulletin. Please take it home, fill it out, and pray about your priorities. Ask God if there are any you need to change."

If it is used as an activity in a small group or as the introduction to the sermon, distribute the sheets at an appropriate time. Close with the comment, "Remember, all answers are completely confidential, so be completely honest with God."

Place a check mark under the response that best describes how this activity ranks in your personal priorities. Then make a second checkmark or an X for conclusions an observer would make based on the amount of time you spend on each activity.

	ALWAYS FIRST	MOST OF THE TIME	NOT IMPORTANT
1) Getting to work on time	_____	_____	_____
2) Time with family	_____	_____	_____
3) Reading the Bible	_____	_____	_____
4) My recreation or hobbies	_____	_____	_____
5) Using my gifts at church or for others	_____	_____	_____
6) Sharing the gospel	_____	_____	_____
7) Helping spouse	_____	_____	_____
8) Praying for missionaries	_____	_____	_____
9) Listening to God's call	_____	_____	_____
10) Available to people who need help or hospitality	_____	_____	_____

Explain that papers will not be shared with anyone else. They are between the individual and God. But help them to see that, often, people put work or their own pleasure/recreation/hobbies as priorities and God's work as less important. Ask them why they couldn't put God's work equal to or above the things of the world. Stress the importance of work, the importance of the family, but that God's work, even missions, need not take a back seat. Encourage everyone to check their priorities. Share the verse, "But seek ye first the kingdom of God and his righteousness, and all these things shall be added unto you" (Matthew 6:33).

Use this idea with the whole congregation as an introduction to the sermon, as an insert in the bulletin, or as a small group activity.

Projected Results:

People will think through their priorities and be reminded of their need to put the Lord and His work Always First, but understand that that doesn't ever mean neglecting one's work or family.

GEOGRAPHY KNOW-HOW

PURPOSE:

To help the people within the congregation know where their missionaries are serving.

PREPARATION:

Prepare a large world map, mount it on plywood, fiber board, or heavy cardboard. Print the name and country of every missionary on separate small cards.

SUPPLIES NEEDED:

❑ Large map
❑ Glue or staple gun
❑ Thumb tacks
❑ Plywood, fiber board or heavy cardboard
❑ Names of all missionaries and their countries
❑ Small cards

TIME NEEDED:

2 minutes per service for as many weeks as necessary to include every missionary. Keep it brief.

WHAT TO DO:

Place the missionary map in the front of the room before the service begins. At the proper moment during the service, have someone with a booming voice announce:

"Today's missionary family is Jonathan Pierce, Jane Pierce, and their 3-month old son, Zachary. They serve in Kenya as evangelists and church planting missionaries among the native people.

The person thumbtacks the name to the proper place on the map. Then he leads the congregation in a brief and simple prayer such as this:

"Father, we thank you for calling the Pierces to serve you on a foreign mission field. We thank you for the privilege you have given to us of helping to support them financially, emotionally, and in prayer. Please help the Pierces as they serve you in Kenya. Meet their needs for good health for Zachary and to learn the native language. Help them not to be home sick. May they see the fruit of your work through them in changed lives. Help us to remember to pray for them. In Jesus' Name. Amen!"

Every week, add another missionary. If there is already an attractive missionary map elsewhere in the church, use this one in the Sunday School area or youth area after it is complete.

This idea can be used in the morning service or during a weekly missionary moment until all the church-supported missionaries are located for the congregation.

Projected Results:

People will see where their missionaries serve. There will be excitement about the missionary of the day, concerted prayer for them, and people will be more apt to pray for the missionaries as they understand where in the world they are serving.

IdEA

41

Once Again for Missions

Purpose:

To help Christians see a way they can do a little more for the cause of missions at home and around the world.

Preparation:

With the pastor's or the missionary committee's help, select one or more missionaries who need a little extra financial, prayer, and/or emotional support. Get a copy of the missionary's prayer card. If possible, get the picture enlarged; the sponsoring mission organization might be able to help with this. Prepare a sheet of paper for the participants with the five questions and signature repeated twice.

Supplies Needed:

- ❑ Copier (or computer and printer)
- ❑ Paper
- ❑ Pencils or pens
- ❑ Posterboard
- ❑ Felt-tip pens
- ❑ Pictures of missionary family
- ❑ Names, addresses, and birthdays of missionary family

Time Needed:

As an ongoing ministry, Once Again for Missions would take 5 minutes the first week and 2 minutes once a month for follow-up.

What to do:

Place the poster with the missionary family picture in front of the meeting place. Let an enthusiastic person explain that there are needs for the family: financial needs, personal needs, and a need for a sense of belonging to a Christian family of believers. Hand out papers that say:

Once Again for Missions

1. I will give $_____ for this missionary family: _____ serving in _____.

2. I will pray daily / weekly for this missionary family.

3. I will write to this special family: _____

4. I will remember the birthdays and other special days of this missionary family: _____,
by doing this: _____

5. I will help this family if and when they have extra needs: _____.

My name: _____

Add: Name of missionaries, address, country of service, area of ministry emphasis, birthdays, wedding anniversary if this is a couple or anniversary of date he/she arrived in the country of service if the missionary is single.

Ask the people to write down what they could and would do to help the family or missionary. Explain that most of the people are already giving to the church and to missions, but maybe another $.50 or $1.00 a week would help the missionaries in a special way. Keep a special account for each missionary and collect the money until ready to send a gift or the money itself.

Ask for specific commitments: Would they pray specifically for this family? Would they write to this person? Would they take a special interest in one of the children? Would they remember their birthdays? Would they send a token of love monthly, quarterly, annually?

Finally, have them sign their names. Tear the paper in half and have the individuals keep one section for themselves and hand in one section. Make a report once a month on the funds that have come in, ask for and count the number of letters sent, ask for a show of hands for people who prayed at home for this particular family. Try to give one significant fact about their ministry at this two minute follow-up.

Projected Results:

Once Again for Missions will help the people see that they can do a little more, and if a whole class does a little more, there will be significant help to a family that is lonely, tired, overworked, and far from home and family.

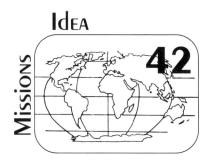

Idea

42

Missions

Pastor's Privilege

Purpose:

To give the pastor the joy of speaking to every class in the Sunday School, the youth groups, and the mid-week clubs about ways to serve the Lord as a missionary. To give the people renewed enthusiasm when they see the pastor's commitment to and involvement in missions.

Preparation:

Ask the pastor to develop a brief, illustrated missionary challenge to present personally in every church-connected class or group.

Supplies Needed:

❑ A willing pastor
❑ Visuals
❑ Time commitment

Time Needed:

5 minutes per presentation over several months

What to do:

The missionary committee may work with the pastor to provide information and help him develop short, illustrated messages which are age appropriate for the little children, the grade school children, the young people, and the adults. Together, the committee and the pastor should list all the groups to be visited and present two, three, or four messages a week until all have been reached. The message should be illustrated (multi-media is a great tool) and perhaps be based on Acts 1:8 or Mark 16:15,20.

The visuals could include:
1) A picture of an open Bible with a Bible verse printed in large letters.

2) Slides of the country and people involved with a voice-over explanation and challenge.

3) A picture of a neighborhood and/or the local community.

4) A map of a nearby state with needs written on arrows pointing to various locations.

5) Pictures of an inner city with people in need.

6) Videotape of a country and the people or children in need narrated by the pastor.

7) Pictures of people and places at home or abroad with "YOU CAN BE A MISSIONARY IN ONE OF THESE PLACES" written on each.

8) Ask the people if they are willing to be a missionary. It must be a brief challenge. Remind them that God has commanded each of them to witness to others about Jesus Christ and their need of salvation. Ask them if they are willing to obey that command. Ask, too, if they are willing to listen for God's special call that may lead them into full-time overseas ministry or service on mission fields within your own country.

The presentations should be announced from the pulpit with words such as, "Soon the pastor will be going to your class with an important message. Be sure to be there to welcome him and hear what he has to say."

Projected Results:

All the classes will get to know the pastor in a special way. They will hear the message of missions in a unique way and may feel the Holy Spirit convicting them to respond to the call.

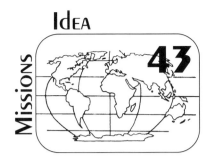

Idea

43

Missions

Round-Robin Sunday School Morning

Purpose:

To let the adults who attend Sunday School classes meet, interact, and get to know the missionaries in person.

Preparation:

Someone to set up a schedule and generate excitement about the missionaries' presence. Inform the Sunday School teachers of the interruption which will occur during the course of the morning so they will be prepared.

Supplies Needed:

❑ Willing pastor
❑ Involved Sunday School teachers
❑ 3-4 visiting missionaries

Time Needed:

10 minutes per missionary per class
5 minutes for missionaries to change classrooms

What to do:

Set up a "round-robin" type program. If there are four missionaries available, have each one attend a different class at a different time, and rotate every ten minutes.

For Example:		
Missionary A	in Senior Adult class	9:45 A.M.
	in Adult class	10:00 A.M.
	in High School class	10:15 A.M.
	in Career Singles class	10:30 A.M.
Missionary B	in Adult class	9:45 A.M.
	in High School class	10:00 A.M.
	in Career Singles class	10:15 A.M.
	in Senior Adult class	10:30 A.M.

Missionary C	in High School class	9:45 A.M.
	in Career Singles class	10:00 A.M.
	in Senior Adult class	10:15 A.M.
	in Adult class	10:30 A.M.
Missionary D	in Career Singles class	9:45 A.M.
	in Senior Adult class	10:00 A.M.
	in Adult class	10:15 A.M.
	in High School class	10:30 A.M.

Ask the missionary to tell briefly of what the focus of their ministry involves, what a day's work might involve, and challenge the people in ways they can be involved.

This idea works well during a missionary conference or missionary emphasis weekend when you have missionaries readily available to the church who would be willing to visit the adult classes.

Projected Results:

Gives adults a world-wide view of missions throughout the church in one Sunday morning.

IdEA

Missions

44

Better Books

Purpose:

To interest the church people in missionary books and/or to provide contemporary Christian books for missionaries whose access to such encouragement is sometimes very limited.

Preparation:

Visit a Christian bookstore, talk with the pastor, visit the church library. Compile two lists of book titles if you choose to do the optional part of this activity - missionary stories to read and contemporary Christian books the missionaries might like to read. Make a poster for the rear of the church for people to sign as they read.

Alert the library staff to expect a larger number of people in to borrow books and offer to help make the missionary book section more noticeable or appealing. Develop an insert for the church bulletin.

Supplies Needed:

❑ Copier (or computer and printer)
❑ Paper
❑ Book lists
❑ People to stuff bulletins
❑ Posterboard
❑ Felt-tip pens
❑ Book display
❑ Book room or drop-off box, optional

Time Needed:

1-2 hours to stuff bulletins (depending on number of bulletins). 10 seconds the week the flyer is in the bulletin and a monthly reminder.
1-2 hours for volunteers to spend checking out the titles at a local Christian bookstore and visiting the church library to compile a list of titles.

What to do:

Make a flyer for a bulletin insert. List at least ten missionary books that would be exciting for people to read.

Include older books like biographies of Hudson Taylor, C. Studd, Mary Slessor, David Livingston, Corrie ten Boom, George Meuller, Adoniram Judson, Borden of Yale. Also include newer books like John and Betty Stam by Kathleen White. Through Gates of Splendor by Elizabeth Elliot is an enduring testimony of God's power, and Isabel Kuhn has written many missionary books. Be sure to include children's missionary books like those by Faith Cox Bailey.

Place the poster near the missionary book display. Ask people to sign their name under each book they read from the current list. In two months, present a certificate to the three who read the most missionary books. Add books to the list every month and let it be an ongoing affair! Financing can come from the Sunday School, from book donations (after careful scrutiny), from special monetary gifts, or from the pastor's library.

Option: Collect money to buy contemporary Christian books to send to missionaries. Shop from discount book catalogues; get donations from personal libraries. Make another poster with a list of suggested books to buy for the missionaries. Ask people to sign their name under each book they will provide for the missionaries. Check the books off as they are bought and/or donated. Prepare a central collection box or room where books for missionaries can be dropped off. Collect money to pay for postage. When you have 5-10 books, box them up and ship them. Air mail is best although more expensive. Check out the customs requirements so that if the missionary must pay duty taxes to get the package, the class can send that money ahead. Or give books to a missionary home on furlough and save postage.

Projected Results:

A reading people, an informed group of believers with an awareness of great missionaries, renewed excitement about missions, and happy missionaries with Better Books in their libraries.

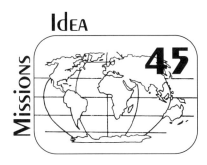

IdEA 45

Excuses for Jesus

Purpose:

To show the hundreds of silly reasons people have for not going, for not giving, for not praying.

Preparation:

Copy (or make) the excuses chart; have enough for everyone to use as a take-home family project.

Supplies Needed:

❑ Copier (or computer and printer)
❑ Paper

Time Needed:

First week—3 minutes
Second week—10-15 minutes

What to do:

Hand out the papers and ask the individuals to fill-in, at home, as many excuses as they can think of for each category. These may not necessarily be their own, but can also include what others might give as an excuse. The take-home paper could look like this:

EXCUSES FOR NOT GIVING TO MISSIONS	EXCUSES FOR NOT PRAYING FOR MISSIONS	EXCUSES FOR NOT GOING TO MISSION FIELD

Instructions: List as many reasons as you can think of, not necessarily your own reasons, but what other people might use. The person with the most reasons will win a prize next week.

At the next meeting, let people read their lists. Expect laughter because some of the reasons will be ridiculous. Then finish the time with a simple question, "What's Your Excuse?" and close in prayer.

Projected Results:

The participants will realize that excuses are not valid; everyone must get involved in missions.

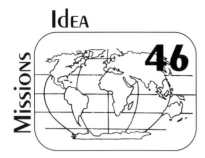

IdEA

Missions

46

Make a Map

Purpose:

To make missions real by locating the missionaries supported by the local church.

Preparation:

Make an outline map of the world; it can be traced from a large world map. Outline the countries where your missionaries are serving. Before each time together, know the country where the missionary of the week is located. Discover some the special needs of that missionary family. Select someone to work on the map during class.

Supplies Needed:

❑ List of church-supported missionaries and the countries where they serve
❑ Bulletin board
❑ Outline map of the world
❑ Large posterboard
❑ Felt-tip pens
❑ Pencils, regular and colored

Time Needed:

3 minutes per group meeting for the number of sessions it takes to go through the list of missionaries

What to do:

Place a list of the church-supported missionaries on a bulletin board. Number them.

At the proper time in the session, ask someone to come to the world map, identify the country's outline, and color in the outline of the country. Then, with a felt-tip pen, print the name of the country and the missionary's name in the proper place on the map. Note any special needs. Have prayer for that missionary and family.

Occasionally, review each missionary already on the map.

Projected Results:

The group members will get to know exactly where the countries are, the missionary families, and have a visual of the needs where they work. They will see the map each week for many weeks and, with encouragement, they will begin to pray at home for the missionary's needs.

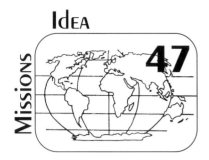

Idea
47

Missions

Quarterly Sermon

Purpose:

To keep the biblical mandate for missions, witnessing, and our obligation to reach out to others with the message of salvation before the people on a regular basis, with the cooperation of the pastor.

Preparation:

Meet with the pastor and ask him to consider including a missionary/witnessing/outreach sermon at least once each quarter. Help the pastor by collecting illustrations and prayer needs of the church missionaries. Advertise the Quarterly Sermon in several ways.

Supplies Needed:

❑ A willing pastor
❑ Up-to-date information

Time Needed:

Approximately 30-45 minutes, once a quarter

What to do:

Ask the pastor to include a missionary sermon once each quarter over and above any missionary speakers who come to share with the church. A good time to include this would be each month that has a fifth Sunday.

Suggestions to help the pastor:
1) Have an "investigator" who would be willing to collect prayer needs and exciting missionary illustrations to help the pastor. Give those to him once a month in writing to help in his preparation, but never tie the pastor's hands on what to preach.

2) Have volunteers the pastor can call upon who would be willing to "illustrate" the sermon by appearing as missionaries or natives to emphasize a point during the pastor's message.

The missions committee ought to devote much time in prayer (at least one full meeting each quarter) both before and after the Quarterly Sermon.

Projected Results:

A church, vibrant with giving, with prayer, and with some going as short-term or long-term missionaries. They will also know the pastor is committed to supporting the efforts of missionaries and involved in their growth as participants in the Great Commission.

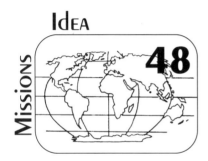

IdEA

Missions

48

No Weak Links

Purpose:

To encourage the people to pray specifically for each need of the missionaries as they become known through a behind the scenes prayer chain organized by one or two people on the missionary committee.

Preparation:

Arrange for a few minutes at a missionary program. Ask for a volunteer to present the idea who will convey the enthusiasm and commitment the idea needs.

Supplies Needed:

❑ Paper and pen on a clipboard, available at the rear of the church
❑ Willing people with telephones

Time Needed:

5 minutes initially; then a continuing commitment

What to do:

The missionary committee should present the feasibility of a Missionary Prayer Line to the group. Whenever anyone on the missionary committee, or any person in the church, receives a prayer request from a missionary, it is channeled through the chairman of the prayer line. That person keeps a list of people willing to pray specifically for these needs.

Before the service, place a table and two volunteers at the back of the room with a sign up sheet that asks for names and phone numbers of those willing to pray. During a meeting, suggest to the group or congregation the needs on the mission field. Say something like this:

"Each time a request comes to our attention, we want to present it quickly to those who are interested in being part of a prayer chain for missionaries. If you would be willing to pray, willing to receive a call and make one call to facilitate the process, please sign up at the back table after the service. We will be in touch as soon as our list is complete."

Take the names and telephone numbers, place them on a list, and number them. Also list the church missionaries on the bottom of the list, along with their place of service, to help the people remember those in whom the church has a special interest. Give a list to each person who signed up.

When a request comes through, the chairman calls number one on the list with the special need. Number one phones number two, etc. through the entire list. Keep the prayer line active. Usually prayer letters arrive every month; some come every week. Someone on the committee should cull the letters, determine any requests or needs, and get it out immediately. When an urgent need is known, make another, special prayer line call. Never let more than a week go by without a request being sent out to the people. But try not to call people every day. Twice a week perhaps should be the limit, once a week the ideal.

Projected Results:

A church that will pray specifically for individuals with real needs and more than just "God bless all the missionaries."

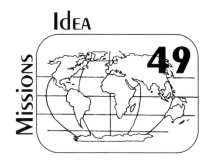

Pass-the-Buck

Purpose:

To show what just a dollar can do in a particular missions endeavor.

Preparation:

Make and send invitations to a church social hour. Find play money; make puzzles out of it. (Cut each play bill into six uneven pieces and clip together.) Prepare at least one play bill puzzle per person. Prepare a list of what a buck can do for missions. Have at least five play dollars for every one present that isn't cut up.

Supplies Needed:

- ❏ Play money
- ❏ Refreshments (cake with money decorations)
- ❏ Invitations
- ❏ Paste
- ❏ Stamps
- ❏ Paper
- ❏ Pencils
- ❏ Copier (or computer and printer)
- ❏ Bell
- ❏ Real dollar bill
- ❏ Tape player
- ❏ Music tape
- ❏ 10 items that each cost a dollar (e.g. pad of paper, pen, cookies, bag of candy, etc)
- ❏ Tray
- ❏ 5 small prizes that cost a dollar each

Time Needed:

1 1/2 hours

What to do:

As people arrive, hand them five play dollar bills. Tell them, "Every time you say "yes" or ""no" you must give a fake dollar to the person who got you to say the word. About half-way through the party, see who has the most money and give that person a prize.

Lead the group in five games.
1) LISTS—
Give everyone paper and pencils. At the ring of a bell, have guests write on one side of the paper as many things as they can think of that money can buy. On the back of the paper, list as many things as they can think of that money can't buy. After five minutes, have them count the items on their lists. The one with the most can read the list. Have the others add any from their lists that are not on the one read. A prize can be given to the one with the most.

2) UNSCRAMBLE—
Distribute a sheet with the following scrambled words on it. Give group five minutes to unscramble them.

1. H C S A
2. B K U S C
3. E L W A H T
4. S R E I H C
5. R R E E T A S U
6. D F N U S
7. L D L O R S A
8. O M N Y E
9. N I E R A O I L M I L
10. F S I E N C A N

Answers: 1) cash, 2) bucks, 3) wealth, 4) riches, 5) treasure, 6) funds, 7) dollars, 8) money, 9) millionaire, 10) finances.

3) PASS-THE-BUCK—
Similar to Musical Chairs, have the group sit in a circle and "Pass-the-Buck" (a real dollar bill) around the room until the music stops. The person with the money must drop out of the game, and it continues until there is only one person left, the winner of the dollar.

4) REMEMBER THE BUCK—
Place ten items that cost a dollar on a tray (e.g. pad of paper, pen, pack of gum, cookies, bag of candy, etc). Let the guests study the tray for 60 seconds. Hide it and let them see how many they can remember by writing them down on a piece of paper. The winners can receive a prize (perhaps the candy or cookies on the tray).

5) PASS-THE-BUCK PUZZLE—
Hand out the previously made money puzzles. At the ring of a bell, let the participants put their puzzle together and paste it on background paper that has the

title, PASS-THE-BUCK at the top, and the words, "GOD LOVES A CHEERFUL GIVER" (II Corinthians 9:7) at the bottom. Give a prize to the first one finished.

Devotions for the social—
"God Loves A Cheerful Giver" and God can use even a dollar. List ways to help with missions via a single dollar. Finally, mention a special "buck" need (possibly close to home) and ask the people to Pass-the-Buck and put what they can into a basket. Pray for the success of the mission project.

Projected Results:

A fun lesson that everyone can identify with and see how even a little money can contribute to the work of the Lord.

Idea

Missions

50

More than a Conference

Purpose:

To immerse believers in the work of missions for one or two days at a one-church or a several-churches missions retreat.

Preparation:

Work with the pastor, select a place, prepare a budget and arrange a way to finance the 1-2 days, secure a dynamic speaker with a proven heart for missions, make invitations and mail one to every adult in the church, invite people personally, plan and make out a schedule.

Supplies Needed:

☐ A retreat center or camp
☐ Bedding items
☐ Notebooks or paper
☐ Pens
☐ Treasurer
☐ Music leader
☐ Food committee
☐ Food supplies
☐ Cook and kitchen crew
☐ Speaker committee
☐ Speaker
☐ Publicity committee
☐ Programs
☐ Exercise/Recreation leader
☐ Sports equipment
☐ Game ideas, including ice-breakers

Time Needed:

Friday night and Saturday

What to do:

Form a committee to select the speaker and plan the schedule. Form another committee to oversee the meals, including purchasing the food, preparing the meals, and serving them. Have another committee responsible for making the invitations, inviting other churches, and handling all the publicity. Make sure the pastor has input. if at all possible in the planning. Use one of the church-supported missionaries as the speaker if possible.

A possible program could be:

Friday Night:
7:00 p.m.	Arrival, get settled
8:00 p.m.	Missionary Rally
8:45 p.m.	Refreshments and fellowship
9:30 p.m.	Small group prayer meetings for missions

Saturday:
7:30 a.m.	Rise and Shine
8:15 a.m.	Breakfast
9:15 a.m.	Missionary Meeting #1
10:15 a.m.	Coffee Break
10:30 a.m.	Exercises
11:00 a.m.	Missionary Story-telling Meeting #2
12:00 Noon	Lunch
1:00 p.m.	Relaxation
1:30 p.m.	Sports events
3:00 p.m.	Final Missionary Meeting #3
4:00 p.m.	Snack
4:30 p.m.	Head for home

Encourage the missionary speaker to include several important elements in his or her presentations such as:
1) Visuals.
2) Challenges for short-term missions, for financial involvement, for serious, daily prayer, for special concrete expressions of love and support for missionaries at home and abroad.
3) Excitement in voice and in truthful presentation of the ministry generated by real life story-telling.

Projected Results:

A congregation that is better informed, more able to pray, open to receive the call of God to serve in a mission field far or near, and a new sense of fellowship and friendship.

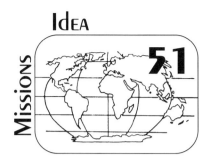

IDEA

51

Missions Ready to Go

Purpose:

To encourage adults and young people to serve as missionaries near home or far away.

Preparation:

Form a small group of missions-minded adults (perhaps the Missions Committees, perhaps a Missions Prayer Group) to excite people to get involved. Meet together to go over plans.

Supplies Needed:

- ❑ People
- ❑ Prayer
- ❑ Flyers from mission boards
- ❑ Posters

Time Needed:

Several weeks

What to do:

The small group needs to meet to 1) Define the needs; 2) Plan ways to excite people (young and old) to serve as missionaries; 3) Provide information about Christian service in various areas; 4) Take some of those interested through the various steps and into an actual place of service.

With the pastor's help, select several areas where people are needed: 1) close to home like a homeless shelter or a nursing home; 2) a place elsewhere in the country where short-term helpers are needed; 3) for overseas challenges both long and short term.

Arrange to visit several youth and adult Sunday School classes to present a fascinating program about serving

God as fully committed partners in the Great Commission. Show posters, printed material, and role play the need for volunteers for a summer, for a month, for a year, for a lifetime. Make the challenge of serving the Lord clearly the most important thing in life. Provide sign-up cards for those with even a slight interest.

Gather those who indicate any interest to a home meeting with the pastor to encourage and once again share the needs. Help those present to evaluate the organizations and opportunities for service at home and abroad, for long or short term programs. Help with applications and go with those interested in nearby projects. Remind people that sometimes just being the "nanny" for two weeks can free a missionary couple with young children to make trips into remote areas that otherwise would not be possible. Secretarial help can enable missionaries to communicate better. Carpenters and other physical skills can provide buildings that might otherwise never be built.

Projected Results:

An alive church, doing what the early church did— sharing the gospel with everyone! Volunteers helping full-time missionaries carry out their work will give a sense of fulfillment and awareness that God can use any ability fully dedicated to Him in the work of leading others to Christ.

IDEA

Missions

52

Road Map ABCs

PURPOSE:

To involve people in the reach-out process of missions.

PREPARATION:

Invite people to a church social via the church bulletin, posters, telephone calls, personal invitations, and postcard reminders to an evening of munchies, merriment, and missions. Find people willing to take care of refreshments, games, devotions, and prepare puzzles for Game 3.

Supplies Needed:

❑ Copies of list of items for scavenger hunt, one for each person present
❑ Photos of several local areas of ministry opportunities
❑ Several road maps of a nearby city cut into puzzles and clipped together
❑ Specially decorated cake
❑ Coffee, tea, water
❑ Invitations
❑ Papers
❑ Pencils
❑ Chairs
❑ Small prizes
❑ Road-map name cards
❑ Felt-tip pens

TIME NEEDED:

1 1/2 - 2 hours

WHAT TO DO:

As the people arrive at the social, give them a name card to wear made from a piece of a road map and a felt-tip pen to write their names.

Game 1—SCAVENGER

Begin while everyone is arriving by giving them a paper with scavenger items to find:

1) Autograph from someone who has helped in any way at a mission
2) A salvation tract
3) The birthday of the pastor
4) A Bible verse from Isaiah to encourage people to be missionaries
5) The signature of someone who wrote to a missionary within the last seven days
6) The name of someone who has been able to witness to a neighbor this week
7) A Bible verse telling us to share the gospel
8) A picture of a home missionary

Game 2—WHERE

Ask guests to sit in a chair in a circle. The leader stands in the center as IT. IT goes to anyone in the circle and says, "You can serve the Lord in..." Then count to 10. That person must answer before the count of 10 or become IT. No place can be mentioned twice. Keep going for approximately 10 minutes. Don't over-extend the game.

Game 3—Puzzles

Take several road maps of a nearby city and, with a marker, write the name of a mission or shelter on each one. Cut the maps into puzzle pieces and clip a complete map together. Divide into teams of three or four and see which group can put the puzzle together first.

Game 4—LISTS

Give everyone paper and pencils. At the count of 3, each one is to list things that can be done by volunteers at a mission or a shelter. The person with the longest list is the winner.

Game 5—I WANT TO HELP ABCs

Have everyone sit in a circle. Explain that the first reply to the question must begin with the letter A. The next person must use the next letter in the alphabet and so on. Have a leader begin by stating, "I want to help in missions because..." A possible answer would be: "I'm aware of the needs."

The person next to the leader repeats the first sentence but adds a reason beginning with 'B': "I want to help in missions because... I'm aware of the needs and because I want to bear their burdens." Keep going around the room, with each person saying the previous sentences plus adding their own. If they can't remember, they become a third of a nerd. No one drops out.

Game 6—LOOK-OUT!

The leader displays a tray of photos that show places to serve the Lord within the area. They might be the local rescue mission, your neighborhood, the church's Sunday School classes, a local homeless shelter, a nursing home, Bible clubs, youth meetings, hospital visitation, etc. The group is told to look-out at the cards for two minutes and try to identify the places. Then take the tray away and have the people write down as many of the places to serve the Lord as they can remember.

Give small prizes to winners of the different games.

Devotions Suggestion: Read aloud Acts 1:8 and Colossians 3:17. Go over the photos of places to serve and encourage the people to get involved. Sing a song like "I Will Serve Thee, Because I Love Thee" by Gloria and William Gaither. Have prayer followed by refreshments.

Refreshments should include a decorated cake with the words SERVE ME on it plus a map of the city.

Projected Results:

A conscious awareness of the needs within easy reach of the local church.

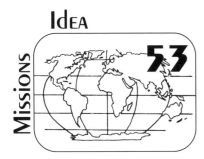

Idea
53

Missions

Scrapbook

Purpose:

To gather missionary literature, to know where to find important information about missions, and to become knowledgeable about the work of missions.

Preparation:

Buy or make a large scrapbook. Have a committee collect literature from many mission agencies.

Supplies Needed:

- ❑ Scrapbook
- ❑ Rubber cement or paste
- ❑ Fine felt-tip pens
- ❑ Scissors
- ❑ Prayer cards
- ❑ Pictures

Time Needed:

Several hours outside of class. A few minutes in class to ask for volunteers and material, and later for showing.

What to do:

Form a committee willing to work on a missions scrapbook. Make a list of what ought to be included, like: Mission organization publicity; church missionaries with pictures, countries, families, addresses, birthdays, etc.; maps and pictures of area people (perhaps from National Geographic or other magazines); short-term missions needs around the world; book and magazine lists.

Outside of class, the committee can place the information into the scrapbook. Ask the class for more information to add to it. Keep it in the class and make it available for easy reference. Display it often in class and in the foyer for all the church to enjoy. Update it at least once a year.

Projected Results:

An educated small group which will influence a whole church, and one that will continue to gain and share their knowledge of the Lord's work around the world.

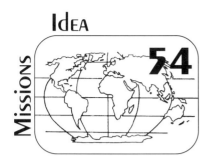

Idea

54

Chaotic Words

PURPOSE:

To encourage missions in a fun, relaxing, educational way.

PREPARATION:

Copy the list of Chaotic Words. Plan a social hour or get-together.

Supplies Needed:

❏ Copies of the Chaotic Words game
❏ Pencils

Time Needed:

10-20 minutes

What to do:

Hand out the Chaotic Words list with pencils. Start at the count of three. Allow the participants about eight minutes to unscramble them.

Chaotic Words

1) O G _____
2) E C T A H _____
3) H H C C U R _____
4) T V N A I E _____
5) N S D E _____
6) E E C I I M D N _____
7) L E B B I _____
8) V E N A E G I L M S _____
9) P H R A E C _____
10) O E S A V R E S _____
11) A N S L A T T R O R _____
12) C O H O L S _____
13) N S E S T I W _____

14) E H P L   _____
15) S M I S I N O   _____
16) M E E O H S L S   _____
17) D A O I R   _____
18) E F E D   _____
19) Y E N O M   _____
20) T L S O   _____

Then ask for volunteers to give an answer and explain what it has to do with missions. Conclude the activity with a brief devotional that challenges people to put these words to practice at home and abroad.

Answers: 1) Go, 2) Teach, 3) Church, 4) Native, 5) Send, 6) Medicine, 7) Bible, 8) Evangelism, 9) Preach, 10) Overseas, 11) Translator, 12) School, 13) Witness, 14) Help, 15) Mission, 16) Homeless, 17) Radio, 18) Feed, 19) Money, 20) Lost.

Projected Results:

Activities based on fun often make a greater impression and stay in the mind longer. The words and the discussion will provide a realization of the broad scope of missionary service as well as give the enjoyment of stretching the mind.

IdEA 55

Missions

Comics Characters & Missions

Purpose:

To present missions to interested adults via comic characters, a fun and instructive media.

Preparation:

Save the comic strips from several Sunday papers. There are some that are more adaptable than others like: Garfield (Jim Davis), Peanuts (Charles M. Schultz), The Born Loser (Art Sansom), Blondie (Young and Drake), or Hagar the Horrible (Chris Browne). Separate each picture frame, cut out the words, and paste the remaining pictures separately on a white piece of light cardboard or paper. Have enough pictures for each participant to have one or two.

Supplies Needed:

- ❑ Colored comic strips
- ❑ Scissors
- ❑ Paste
- ❑ Paper or light cardboard
- ❑ Pens

Time Needed:

1-2 hours to prepare the special cartoons
10-15 minutes following a Bible study or message about missions

What to do:

After a challenging Bible message or missionary message, hand everyone one or two papers containing a single picture from a comic strip. It is not meant to be a continuous story with anyone else's picture, but complete in itself. The participants fill in words about the lesson or message that would cause people to understand or submit to the call of world missions.

After five or six minutes, ask for volunteers to read their words and explain their picture. Some will be comical. Some will be very serious. Some may cause questions worthy of discussion. Take time for as many as possible, but don't force everyone to share. Conclude with a short challenge and place as many as possible on a bulletin board.

A weekday Bible study class or adult Sunday School class or a missions-oriented social would be a good place to use this idea.

Projected Results:

People will think about missions and be challenged by sharing their ideas in a unique, non-threatening way.

IdEA 56

MEdicAl Helps

PuRpOSE:

To help missionaries who have trouble getting enough medical supplies, and to help people see that there are important helps they can contribute other than money.

PREpARATiON:

Select a committee to oversee the project. Contact missionaries who need medicines. Copy lists of needs, local doctors, hospitals, pharmaceutical companies. Make a box for receiving the goods. Make a poster announcing the project.

SuppliEs NEEdEd:

❏ Chairman and committee willing to organize project
❏ Poster to announce and explain the project
❏ Lists of local doctors
❏ Lists of local hospitals
❏ Lists of pharmaceutical companies
❏ Box for collecting supplies
❏ Money to mail gathered supplies

TiME NEEdEd:

30 minutes to write missionaries to get information
5 minutes the first week to launch this ongoing project
1 minute for a couple of weeks
a 3 minute monthly update
30 minutes to package and mail the gathered supplies

WHAT TO do:

Check with several missionaries and discover a place that really needs medicines, bandages, etc. If there is no need, contact an organization like MAP, Medical Assistance Program (Brunswick, GA) or Mexican Medical Mission (San Diego, CA). Ask how the group

117

can get involved with providing medical help to third world countries. You may need a statement from the doctor at the receiving end as to the authenticity of the collection and the recipients qualifications to receive it. Secure that in advance.

Ask people to contact their personal doctor or one or two doctors from the provided list. Ask for samples for medical missions: Vitamins, medicines, antiseptics, dressings, etc. are all needed. If doctors are willing, offer to pick up what they can donate at the end of each month and bring it to the designated place in the church.

Package and mail one box monthly or quarterly to the recipient(s). Be sure the group knows how much is sent, the need for postage money, and always read any correspondence from the missionary or the organization to the whole group. Praise the people for making a difference in the health of needy people and explain how the medical ministry helps on the road that leads to salvation through Christ.

This can be a whole church project, a Bible Study group project, or young adult Sunday School project.

Projected Results:

An interested and praying group of Christians, a witness to the home-based medical community, a better supplied missionary, a need fulfilled that will bring souls to Christ.

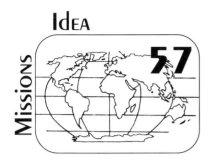

Idea

57

PICTURE EXCHANGE

PURPOSE:

To know church missionaries by sight as well as by name, and to give the missionaries faces of the church people so they can know them.

PREPARATION:

Find missionary addresses, collect prayer cards, plan a special Bible Study or small group meeting to work on the Picture Exchange. Plan a time to share the results with the entire church.

SUPPLIES NEEDED:

❑ Posterboard
❑ Missionaries' prayer cards
❑ Paper
❑ Pens
❑ Rubber cement, glue, or tape
❑ Felt-tip markers, various colors
❑ Pictures of the church people
❑ Copier (or take the finished product to a commercial quality copy shop for a better grade of copies)
❑ Legal-sized paper

TIME NEEDED:

One evening
Time to make the photocopies and mail them

WHAT TO DO:

Announce a special program called Picture Exchange. Ask everyone to bring a picture of themselves, or their family.

When everyone is together,
1) Place all the pictures of church people on a legal-sized white posterboard and number each one. Give everyone paper and pencil.

2) Have everyone write their names and one item of interest about themselves on the paper. Tape or glue those by their pictures.

3) Place all the missionary prayer cards on a sheet of white posterboard, but cover the names. Arrange the pictures attractively and glue (with rubber cement, preferably). Number them. Hand out paper and pencils. Give 5-7 minutes to see how many they can identify.

4) Before you place the missionary pictures' poster in the church foyer have the small group print PICTURE EXCHANGE at the top. Provide colored markers and invite those present to draw interesting designs. Those not drawing can be the peanut gallery and cheer the "artists." (Be sure everyone has an opportunity to add designs.)

5) Have a missionary hymn-sing with five or six missionary songs like, "Jesus Saves," "Christ for the World We Sing," "So Send I You," and "Send the Light."

5) Have someone read Matthew 28:16-20 aloud and Psalm 67.

6) Have a prayer time for the church-supported missionaries and for those willing to help support those called into full-time missions service.

7) Photocopy the pictures of church people. Make one copy for each missionary and one for each person present. Write short notes to the missionaries and enclose the copied pictures.

8) Serve refreshments including a cake with a missionary motif.

Projected Results:

Good fellowship with a two-fold purpose: fun and missions awareness.

Coins for Missions

Purpose:

To show that coins can add up to lots of money. To show that there is always a way to give a little more.

Preparation:

Find the biggest glass jug imaginable. Make a poster. Discover a missionary with a specific need like a car, a computer, or building materials. If you have someone with the creativity, make a cardboard container in the shape of whatever the project is for—computer, car, house, etc. Place the large jar inside it. Ask an enthusiastic person to make a public announcement.

Supplies Needed:

❑ Posterboard
❑ Felt-tip markers
❑ Pictures
❑ Name and address of a missionary and the need
❑ Huge glass bottle with a wide mouth for coins
❑ Coin wrappers
❑ Cardboard replica of item to be purchased, optional

Time Needed:

4-5 minutes the first week
60 seconds in succeeding weeks until the jar is full
1 hour in a group setting to wrap the coins
1 hour for someone to take the money to the bank, get a check in that amount, write a letter, and mail it to the missionary. A fun option would be to mail the cardboard replica also.

What to do:

Select a missionary with a specific, tangible need. Find out how much it will cost to meet that need. An enthusiastic person should make the announcement, perhaps something like this:

"Don and June need a computer to help with their language work. There is no way they can pay for it out of their monthly support. See this huge jar? It will be here in this room every Sunday for the next few weeks. Would you drop extra coins into this jar until it is full? Then we'll empty it and fill it again until we have $_____. It may not pay for the computer completely, but it will get them on the way to purchasing it. Remember, this is Coins for Missions. No paper money, please! Let's see what our coins can do for Jesus."

On succeeding weeks, make short announcements like, "Our Coins for Missions project is working. So far our jar is one-fourth (one-half, one-third, etc.) full. Or, "Be sure to check out all the coins for missions in our jar." Or, "Did anyone forget to bring their coins? See who can change a dollar bill for you." Then give time for those with lots of change to exchange paper money for coins so everyone can contribute. Or, "Empty your pocket change into our Coins for Missions jar as you leave today." Or, if your class is open to it, have them form a line and drop their pocket change into the jar as a group activity.

When the jar is full, have a social hour to count the money, wrap it, and see how near the goal the coins added up to. Sing "The Doxology" together or "To God be the Glory."

It's a good idea to have someone take the money jar home each week. It will create a more personal interest if everyone has an opportunity to share in this responsibility. Be sure the one responsible each week remembers to take it and bring it back the next Sunday.

Option: It may be possible that someone in your class has a computer which can be donated to fill a missionary's need. If so, collect money for the appropriate software—and consider including a game for the missionary's children.

Projected Results:

People will realize, that with just a little effort and a small sacrifice, a special need can be met by giving just a little bit more for God's work each week.

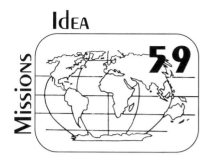

IdEA **59**

Missions

IF I WERE YOU

PURPOSE:

To encourage people to think through the meaning and the application of missions.

PREPARATION:

None

SUPPLIES NEEDED:

❏ An informal area in a home or the church

TIME NEEDED:

15 minutes at most

WHAT TO DO:

The leader should be enthusiastic about missions and able to encourage spirited conversation among the people. Don't let it be a sermon. The conversation might go like this:

Leader: It's great to be together. We have a theme for the next few minutes titled, "If I were you..." Let's begin with God's Word.

Ask someone to read Matthew 9:36-38 aloud. Explain that the person to the right of the leader will begin the discussion, and finish the sentence. After five or six answers, stop the talk and the last person to speak selects someone in the circle to be the first person on the next open sentence. Begin the discussion with the following unended sentences.

1) If I were you, and I heard about a need in Africa, I would...

2) If I were you, and I knew my neighbor was out of work, I would...

3) If I were you, and I heard a sermon about the financial needs of one of our missionaries, I would...

4) If I were you, and I heard about the need for my skills for a short term call, I would...

5) If I were you, and there weren't enough people to serve meals to the elderly and shut-ins, I would...

6) If I were you, and the pastor asked for volunteers to canvas the housing project and bring unchurched people to our church, I would...

7) If I were you, and there was a need to help with our young people, I would...

8) If I were you, and there was a need for workers in Vacation Bible School, I would...

9) If I were you, and a missionary on furlough needed a place to stay, I would...

10) If I were you, and I needed my tithe money for new work clothes, I would...

Conversation can be light or humorous at times, and should not be stifled because everyone is talking about what "others" ought to do!

Finish with a prayer time that each person present will re-evaluate what God might want them to do and people they can help.

This idea works well in a small group atmosphere where people are willing to talk.

Projected Results:

An inward look into excuses people make about serving the Lord at home or abroad often helps people see any blind spots they have about their service. God will speak through these open-ended sentences, if people listen!

Check It Out!

Purpose:

To encourage short-term ministry someplace where there is a need in the world.

Preparation:

Send for literature from mission organizations that use short-term workers both within the country and around the world.

Supplies Needed:

❏ Large map of the world
❏ Missions information
❏ Leader
❏ Missions video

Time Needed:

1 hour

What to do:

Gather the group together and place a large map of the world in front of the group. Or you may want to break it down by having large maps of each continent. Sing some hymns and choruses promoting missions like, "I Will Serve Thee, Because I Love Thee."

Show a video, if possible, like "EE-TAOW!" produced by New Tribes Mission.

Ask someone who has gone on a short-term mission project to share the experience.

Present a list of places and needs around the world that are open to people for service. Ask the pastor or a missions committee member to give a brief message about the "Great Commission" in Matthew 28:19-20. Suggest that people check it out.

Have a time of silent prayer. If possible, try to raise some money so that a group of individuals can go for two weeks or a month. Let those who seem interested get together after the meeting and pray for God's will.

Be sure to follow up the meeting by encouraging those who are interested in going and those who are willing to help financially to get them to the destination God leads.

Finally, have a victory meeting after the short-termer(s) return.

Projected Results:

Actual missionary service and prayer for missions for people they know. Increased concern for the work overseas or missions nearer to home. Perhaps, even more people will Check It Out and decide to help in missions in the future.

Alphabetical Index of Missions Ideas